The Jury: A Very Short Introduction

T0016975

VERY SHORT INTRODUCTIONS are for anyone wanting a stimulating and accessible way into a new subject. They are written by experts, and have been translated into more than 45 different languages.

The series began in 1995, and now covers a wide variety of topics in every discipline. The VSI library currently contains over 700 volumes—a Very Short Introduction to everything from Psychology and Philosophy of Science to American History and Relativity—and continues to grow in every subject area.

Very Short Introductions available now:

For more information visit our website

www.oup.com/vsi/

Renée Lettow Lerner

THE JURY

A Very Short Introduction

OXFORD
UNIVERSITY PRESS

Oxford University Press is a department of the University of Oxford.
It furthers the University's objective of excellence in research, scholarship,
and education by publishing worldwide. Oxford is a registered trade mark of
Oxford University Press in the UK and certain other countries.

Published in the United States of America by Oxford University Press
198 Madison Avenue, New York, NY 10016, United States of America.

© Oxford University Press 2023

Cataloging-in-Publication data is on file at Library of Congress

ISBN 978–0–19–092391–4

Printed and bound by
CPI Group (UK) Ltd, Croydon, CR0 4YY

For Charles Lettow,
who sits without juries but appreciates their history,
and in memory of Sue Lettow

Contents

List of illustrations

The Jury

Acknowledgments

I owe a great debt to the many jurors, judges, lawyers, trial consultants, historians, and academics around the world from whom I have had the pleasure of learning about the jury.

Traci Emerson Spackey of the George Washington University Law Library provided extraordinarily creative and effective help in locating images and other sources. Clifford Ando gave valuable recommendations about sources for the ancient world, and Daniela Cammack kindly provided drafts of her now-published article about Athenian juries. Trial lawyer Bobby Burchfield gave detailed and deeply knowledgeable comments on the manuscript. Karen Wahl provided expert assistance locating sources. I thank Morgan Reinhardt for allowing me to use her research on jury forepersons, and Anna Offit, her law professor, for guiding me to her and for comparative work on juries. Anna Caraveli and Jonathan Chaves, my colleague at George Washington University, made important suggestions and pointed out places in which non-lawyers needed further explanation of legal concepts. My daughter Anna Lerner provided the perspective of a younger reader and gently let her mother know where improvements would be helpful. For decades, John Langbein has been a constant source of insight about juries. I am grateful to Akhil Amar for first sparking, and then encouraging, my interest in the subject, and for his vibrant work. My husband, Craig Lerner, gave unceasing encouragement and invaluable advice.

Introduction

Two well-known movies about the jury, made five years apart, portray the institution very differently. In the 1957 film *12 Angry Men*, jurors in New York City have to decide on the guilt of an eighteen-year-old charged with murder. The judge tells the jurors that if they convict, the sentence will be death. The verdict must be unanimous. After the first three minutes in the courtroom, the rest of the movie shows the deliberations in the jury room. At first, the jurors are convinced that the evidence is overwhelming, and all vote to convict in an initial vote—except one. Heroic Juror 8, played by Henry Fonda, persuades his fellow jurors to deliberate thoroughly. In the process, the jurors reveal their different personalities and backgrounds and scrutinize each bit of evidence. They examine a diagram of a witness's apartment and conduct an experiment, timing the witness's alleged movements to see whether they match his testimony. An immigrant juror tells the others: "We have a responsibility. This is a remarkable thing about democracy." After hours of deliberation, the jurors all vote to acquit.

The American Film Institute chose *12 Angry Men* as the second-best courtroom drama of all time. The best was the 1962 movie *To Kill a Mockingbird*. That film is based on a novel of the same name by Harper Lee and is set in the fictional town of Maycomb, Alabama, during the early 1930s. Lawyer Atticus Finch, played by Gregory Peck, is defense counsel for Tom Robinson, a Black man accused of raping a white woman. Atticus talks to his young son about "what real courage is.... It's when you know you're licked before you begin, but you begin anyway and see it through no matter what." Atticus knows he is defeated before the trial even begins because no jury at that time and place would acquit a Black defendant of such a crime. The jury is all-white, as Black people were systematically excluded. At trial, Atticus destroys the prosecution's case, but the jury convicts nevertheless.

The jury can be inspiring, even romantic. "We the jury" is the stuff of novels, movies, shows, and video games. The word conjures images of Magna Carta, liberty, self-rule, the wisdom of crowds, and ordinary people's common sense serving as a check against self-interested or out-of-touch elites. But the jury also has a dark side. Juries may be biased, or confused by the law and evidence. Citizens do not always welcome a summons for jury service, and many try to get out of jury duty. By necessity, modern legal systems are set up on a professional basis, with the need to decide complicated questions of fact and some aspiration to apply the law in an accurate, predictable way.

This book will show how many societies around the world, ancient and modern, have used lay juries, and how they have tried to resolve the tension always present between predictable law and popular justice. This tension has grown over time because of greater specialization and knowledge. Often specialists—lawyers and judges—have co-opted juries for their own purposes. They have used juries as cover for furthering their interests.

Jurors are laypersons, meaning that they are not professional judges. "Lay" comes from the Greek *laikos*, "of the people," as opposed to a member of the clergy or a body of professionals. The word "juror" comes from the French word *jureur*, a person who swears an oath. All jurors take an oath or make an affirmation to decide the case fairly. Professional judges have no need to take an oath in each case. When they became judges, they took the judicial oath of office. Lay jurors have no durable office, and so they need to be sworn, in effect as temporary judges. The oath that jurors take for criminal cases in federal courts in the United States is some version of: "Do each of you solemnly swear (or affirm) that you will well and truly try, and true deliverance make, in the case now on trial and render a true verdict according to the law and the evidence, so help you God?" This oath is close to the one administered to English jurors since the Middle Ages. In the oath, the word "true" appears again and again. In fact, the word "verdict" means a true saying. Such repetition suggests concern.

Although many societies have used juries, the jury as it exists today is a direct descendant of the medieval English jury. The institution is a defining characteristic of what is known as the "common-law system." The common-law system is the name for the family of legal systems used in England and Wales and former British colonies including the United States, Canada, Caribbean countries, African countries, New Zealand, and Australia. Around the world, only former British colonies have adopted the common-law system.

In Europe, the English common-law system was a strange anomaly. The main family of Western European legal systems is known as the "civil-law system." In this context, the civil-law system does not mean a system for dealing with civil cases only; the term refers to the entire legal system, both civil and criminal. The civil-law system developed mainly in the Roman Catholic church and then spread to secular governments. That system traditionally used professional judges instead of lay jurors to decide cases. It is known by other names, including the inquisitorial system, or the Roman-canon system. It has spread around the world to Latin America, Africa, and Asia. A major theme of this book is the contrast between the common-law and civil-law systems.

Many countries with civil-law systems are now trying to use lay decision-makers. They do so almost exclusively in criminal cases.

For democracies or would-be democracies, the use of lay jurors in criminal cases seems nearly irresistible. One form this use has taken is the mixed panel of lay jurors sitting with professional judges.

Ironically, throughout the common-law world the actual use of juries is in steep decline. While non-common-law countries have added lay jurors in criminal cases, common-law countries are replacing criminal jury trial with plea bargaining and non-jury proceedings. And, except for the United States, common-law countries have virtually abolished civil juries.

As Alexis de Tocqueville, the French commentator on American democracy, put it in 1835, "The jury system arose in the infancy of society, at a time when only simple questions of fact were submitted to the courts; and it is no easy task to adapt it to the needs of a highly civilized nation, where the relations between men have multiplied exceedingly and have been thoughtfully elaborated in a learned manner." Many writers quote Tocqueville on the benefits of the jury, but they forget his warning.

The future of the jury will depend on finding ways to incorporate lay decision-makers that are efficient and acceptable to judges and lawyers. Legal professionals have many ways to subvert lay participation in deciding cases, if they find it in their interest to do so. Clearly, however, there remains a strong popular sense in many countries that lay participation in deciding criminal cases is desirable or necessary. Working out ways to incorporate lay decision-makers into criminal cases seems worth the considerable challenge.

Chapter 1
Why use lay jurors? The ancient and medieval world

Societies at different times and places have had various reasons for using lay jurors. Ancient societies had to find ways to cope with a huge divide: that between the few and the many. In most of these societies, a small and often hereditary elite enjoyed concentrated wealth and power. This elite provided order, learning, and continuity in the state. Meanwhile, the vast majority of people who were not enslaved produced goods and services as small farmers, hired laborers, servants, or craft workers. Each of these groups could threaten the other. The few could oppress the many, but the many had numbers and thus power on their side, if they acted together. The resulting conflict in society could produce instability and eventually chaos and dissolution, often by conquest from outside. For society to flourish, or even continue, the few and the many had to reconcile.

Athens developed a powerful form of control over elites: the popular jury. The reforms of the statesman Solon in 594 BCE began the development of popular juries that continued right up until Macedonia ended the Athenian democracy in 322 BCE. For many Athenians, the jury was an important element—perhaps the key element—of Athenian democracy. Ancient Athenians considered these juries a more potent form of the people's power than even the popular assembly, which elites could more easily manipulate. In his *Politics*, Aristotle stressed the Athenian people's control of the courts as the main source of its power. The orator Demosthenes argued that juries were the only protection the people had against oppression by the elite.

Such was the popular Athenian attachment to juries that playwrights could not resist poking fun. In Aristophanes' play *The Clouds*, a character looks at a map of Greece and fails to find Athens because no jurors are shown. In his play *The Wasps*, the main character is a down-at-the-heels old man addicted to serving on juries. This character revels in the small daily stipend for jury service—less than a laborer could earn—plus the excitement of hearing a case and the feeling of importance when he votes on the decision.

Athenian popular juries were vastly different from modern juries in their composition and discretion. The Athenian juries were designed to be as direct an expression of the will of the people as possible. Jury service was open to all male citizens thirty years or older. Each year, a judicial roll of 6,000 potential jurors was chosen by lot from volunteers. Once selected for the judicial roll, the citizens swore the judicial oath and received an official name plate. Over time, the selection of jurors for cases was randomized. Each court day, those who wanted to serve as jurors showed up outside the courts at dawn and handed in their name plates. Jurors would then be chosen for particular cases by lot. Between 200 and 1,500 jurors decided a case, depending on the subject. On any given court day, between 1,000 and 2,000 total jurors were needed. Neither the litigants nor the magistrate could remove any jurors from the panel; there was no mechanism for striking or questioning jurors. The large numbers and random selection occurring on the day of decision made it difficult for parties to bribe, intimidate, or pack the jury.

The jurors decided an enormous range of cases. These included trials of persons who had public responsibilities for misusing authority. Jurors did not spare leading citizens. Athenian politicians spent a lot of time defending themselves in court, and virtually all important politicians were convicted of something at some point. Even Pericles, the leader of Athens during its golden age and the beginning of the Peloponnesian War with Sparta, was accused of theft, convicted, stripped of his generalship, and heavily fined. The people reinstated him soon after, but they had made the point that they were in control.

Perhaps the most famous Athenian convicted in a popular court was not a politician but a philosopher—Socrates. In 399 BCE, Socrates was accused of impiety and of corrupting the youth. According to Plato, in his defense Socrates tried "to teach and to persuade" the jurors about the true nature of justice and judging. His attempt failed, as the jurors narrowly convicted him. Next each side proposed a punishment. At first, Socrates suggested that he receive meals at the public expense, but he ended by arguing for a small fine. The jurors were not amused. They overwhelmingly adopted the prosecutors' proposal: death.

The amount of discretion afforded these jurors is astounding. In each case, there was a trial-like proceeding with evidence. No case could last longer than a day. But, within those constraints, the litigants were almost entirely free to present any evidence they liked. A litigant's prior military service, the generosity of his family to the city, his or his family's reputation—all were fair game. Litigants even brought weeping children onto the speaking platform.

Not only did the jurors hear all sorts of evidence and have the ability to make of it what they would, but they were almost entirely free to decide questions of law. The laws of Athens were notoriously vague; they did not define the elements of a crime. An example is a law of 410 BCE: "If anyone wrongs the people of Athens, then that man, while chained up, is to be tried before the people, and if he is found guilty, he is to be killed by being thrown into a pit and his money confiscated and a tithe to be given to the goddess."

It was wholly up to the jurors to decide what wronging the people meant, just as it was up to them to decide what was treason, or impiety, or corrupting the youth.

Immediately after both sides presented their cases, the jurors voted. They did not formally discuss the case, or as we would say deliberate, at all. This was to prevent an effective orator among the jurors—or simply peer pressure—from swaying the votes. The idea was that each juror should decide for himself free from influence, so that the verdict would reflect the sum of each juror's independent opinion.

Juror voting was by secret ballot, and the courts used procedures carefully designed to ensure that secrecy. The method evolved over time. By 345 BCE, each juror had two small bronze ballots, one with a hollow axle representing a verdict for the prosecutor and one with a solid axle representing a verdict for the defendant. The juror dropped his vote into a bronze urn and the discard into a wooden urn. With the ballot held between the juror's thumb and forefinger, it was impossible for an observer to tell which was which.

A majority of votes sufficed to convict. Following a conviction, the jury heard additional speeches and decided on punishment, if the law or decree did not specify it. There were no appeals from the decision of the jury.

1. These Athenian jurors' bronze ballots date from the fourth century BCE. Jurors used the ballot with a hollow axle to vote for the prosecutor, and the ballot with a solid axle to vote for the defendant.

This way of deciding cases is far from modern notions of the rule of law. Most of us prefer our laws to be more precise and their application more predictable. Precision and predictability were not the goal of the Athenians in the popular courts. It is fair to say that Athenian juries were one of the most radical expressions of democracy the world has ever known. The discretion of jurors was so great that the Greek word for jurors, *dikastai*, is translated as both "jurors" and "judges," often interchangeably by the same translator. The Athenian idea was that a wrong was whatever most people at the time thought it was. Discovering what most people thought at any given time was the purpose of the huge, randomly selected juries, enormous discretion over fact and law, and secret ballots with no appeal.

The Athenian jury thus represents an extreme pole on a continuum of popular involvement in judicial decision-making. It had the advantage of allowing the people to control powerful elites directly and firmly. It also had disadvantages. Such a free-wheeling idea of law and justice—defined by the people in the moment—made stable, effective government difficult. It also, as the case of Socrates demonstrated, could be used to suppress nonconformist views.

Drawing on local knowledge, on the cheap

Other societies have not had as extreme a view of popular law-making as the ancient Athenians, but they have used ordinary people to decide cases. Traditional societies throughout the world have relied on groups, often an entire village, to pronounce judgment. This was true among the Germanic tribes, in Russia, in China, and in countless other places. Law was customary, built up of practices that had developed over time and that provided stability for the group. Ordinary persons readily understood and could apply these customs. And they were likely to be familiar with the facts, as everyone knew everyone else in these small societies.

It is tempting to view the common-law jury in medieval England as a simple outgrowth of this tradition. But the reality is more complex. The medieval English jury, from which so many modern practices descend, was in fact the result of decisions by Norman kings.

Many myths surround the origins of the English common-law jury, myths that persist among educated people today. Antiquarians and historians attributed the development of the common-law system—and especially the jury—to the Anglo-Saxons. This myth began as far back as the late sixteenth century. In the seventeenth century, opponents of royal absolutism such as the judge and then Member of Parliament Sir Edward Coke eagerly picked up the idea that jury trial and other elements of the common-law system predated the Norman King William's conquest of England in 1066. In the minds of Coke and others, such an early origin meant that the Norman kings and their descendants could not take away the ancient liberties of Englishmen, including jury trial.

This myth caught on in the American colonies in the late eighteenth century as they struggled against British imperial control. Thomas Jefferson took up the theory with his usual enthusiasm, to the point of writing an Anglo-Saxon grammar and recommending that the study of Anglo-Saxon be required at the university he founded, the University of Virginia. In his mind, Anglo-Saxon was the language of liberty. In the nineteenth century, romantic nationalists and advocates of pan-Teutonic solidarity imagined gatherings of free common men under great trees in England and Germany to decide disputes. The myth grew up that the Anglo-Saxons developed the institutions of liberty—including jury trial and Parliament. The myth assigned a black hat: the usurping Norman kings did their best to undermine these free institutions and to substitute their personal, often tyrannical, rule.

But these accounts of Anglo-Saxon liberty and the origins of jury trial were wrong. The common-law jury originated not with the Anglo-Saxons, but with the Norman kings. In fact, with a very French Norman king. If anyone could be said to be the originator of the common law and juries, it was King Henry II (r. 1154–1189).

Henry II represented the polar opposite of the Anglo-Saxon dream so many later cherished. His father was French, he was born in France, and he was mostly raised and educated there. He spoke only French and Latin (though he probably understood English as well). According to chroniclers, he was good-looking, red-haired, and freckled, with a large head and a short, stocky body. He was bow-legged from a life in the saddle. Often he was shoddily dressed. But he was well educated by several prominent academics. He had remarkable energy and drive. His lifelong passion was to regain and cement control over the territory ruled by his grandfather, Henry I of England. In this, against the odds, he succeeded. His judicial reforms were a large part of his success.

When Henry II took the throne in 1154, he faced an administrative and legal disaster. The country had just been through a long period of civil war, aptly called the Anarchy. The royal finances were in shambles, and so was the system of royal justice. Criminal justice had deteriorated. Local lords had seized power from the Crown. Even in normal circumstances, the major forms of criminal accusation and trial had grievous shortcomings. But the Anarchy had magnified their weaknesses.

Before Henry II, the main form of criminal accusation for serious crime was the "appeal of felony." The victim, or a close relative of the victim in the case of a homicide, had to make an individual accusation against a particular person. If the victim and the accused were both men, they had a trial by combat. This was done with swords and shields, and therefore often fatal. If for some reason the accused lost but did not die in the combat, he was immediately executed.

To the modern mind, this method of trial seems baffling. It must be understood as a method of ordeal, in which God was called upon to give judgment to the combatant who was in the right. Henry and others saw that it could be abused. A thug skilled in fighting could take advantage of this system in several ways. He could accuse another falsely, extort a settlement or win the combat, and proceed to intimidate everyone else in the neighborhood. He could also commit crimes with impunity, knowing that no one would dare to accuse him and fight him.

Henry took seriously the king's obligation to dispense justice, particularly after such a period of upheaval. The provision of justice had to improve. But how exactly could criminal justice be fixed?

One possibility was to rely on royal officials—professional judges—to investigate and to collect accusations. The Roman Catholic church had already begun to develop such a system. But this system did not reach England, through the church courts, until the 1180s. Henry II needed a method he could use immediately, in the 1160s, when he was trying to consolidate power and to rebuild the administration of justice.

Furthermore, Henry strongly preferred a system that was cheap. He had extensive domains in France as well as his English kingdom to administer, and he was reluctant to spend a lot of money to train and maintain many royal officials if he did not have to. What to do? The solution he and his advisers hit upon was to use groups of local, ordinary persons to make the accusations. Groups of men from the locality, including each village, would be gathered together, put on oath, and forced to say whether anyone was suspected of being a criminal. These men would not be paid. These jurors would make their accusations—known as presentments—mostly before the sheriff of each county, when he presided over the local court twice a year. Later, the name of the accusation was changed to an "indictment." Here is the origin of the grand jury, and indeed of the entire jury system.

Henry and his advisers did not invent the idea of collecting groups of men and putting them on oath to give information. There were precedents, particularly in Germanic kingdoms, for using such groups. These were known as inquests. In the ninth-century Frankish Carolingian empire, such groups were convened to give answers about a range of topics of royal interest, including fiscal matters and military preparedness. The Anglo-Saxon kings of England used similar methods. So did Henry's great-grandfather William the Conqueror, who used this technique to make inquiries about landholding and population that were recorded in the Domesday Book (1086). But these were all ad hoc inquiries, made at particular times to get specific information when needed.

To Henry and his counselors, it was not such a stretch to apply the method of inquest to making criminal accusations. But what was different, Henry's true innovation, was to make these inquests regular and uniform.

This was the beginning of accusation by the public. Group accusation helped to solve the problem of local thugs intimidating individual would-be accusers. This solution also saved the English king's money. Here were ordinary men who were not paid for doing this job. They were fined, though, if they failed to show up or failed to present, that is to accuse, all those who were suspect. The early jury system—and later ones too—relied heavily on coercion and threats.

Henry II announced this procedure in 1166 in a declaration called the Assize of Clarendon. This is the closest thing we have to the official beginning of the common-law jury.

[T]he aforesaid King Henry, on the advice of all his barons, for the preservation of peace, and for the maintenance of justice, has decreed that inquiry shall be made throughout the several counties and throughout the several hundreds [localities] through twelve of the more lawful men of the hundred and through four of the more lawful men of each vill [village] upon oath that they will speak the truth, whether there be in their hundred or vill any man accused or notoriously suspect of being a robber or murderer or thief, or any who is a receiver of robbers or murderers or thieves, since the lord has been king....

It was all very well to start using groups of laypersons to make these accusations. But what guarantee did Henry have that their presentments would be accurate? The first guarantee was the oath that each juror swore. According to Bracton's thirteenth-century law book, this oath ended "so help me God and these holy relics." The oath invoked the juror's Christian faith and the hope of eternal life; the perjury of a false accusation or concealment risked damnation of the juror's immortal soul. The presentment jurors, or juries of accusation, also had incentive because of the threat of being fined if they failed to make an accusation against one who was suspect.

Assuming that the jurors were trying to tell the truth, how would they know who was accused or notoriously suspect? To answer this question, we must imagine a society very different from our own. In our society, next-door neighbors may be virtual strangers. We routinely see dozens, if not hundreds, of strangers every day. In the villages and small towns where these men lived, everyone knew each other and all about each other's business. Many were related by birth or marriage. The vast majority of them were peasant farmers, constantly working together in the same fields. Anything significant happening in the village would almost instantly be known to all. Even the sight of a stranger was rare. Under these conditions, the king and his judges could expect that jurors would be self-informing. The jurors would come into court

2. In an image from an early thirteenth-century German manuscript, a group of sworn men make an accusation against a man shown crouching beside the official receiving the information. The jurors swore on saints' relics, kept in the reliquary on top of the column.

not needing to be given information, but already knowing who was suspected of a crime.

What would happen to someone whom the jury of presentment accused? The accused went to an ordeal. If the accused was a man, he went to the ordeal by cold water. A priest said a special mass to invoke God's judgment. The accused was tied up, put on a boat, and rowed into a lake, river, or pond. He was then let down into the water by a rope. If he sank, he was innocent, as the water had accepted him. If he floated, he was guilty; the pure water had rejected him. Women, because of their higher percentage of body fat, were more likely to float and thus to be found guilty. Possibly for this reason, women were sent to the ordeal of hot iron. Again, the priest held a special mass. During the mass, a bar of iron was heated red-hot. The accused was required to take it in her hand and carry it nine feet. Then the hand would be bandaged and after three days inspected by the priest. If the priest said the hand was healing, the accused was declared innocent; if not, guilty.

15

Hard as it may be to believe, rulers all over Europe used the ordeals as a main method of adjudication. The priest was thought to be able to call on the judgment of God in this manner. And in such a serious matter as a felony case, God's judgment was the only one the people trusted.

But suddenly, in 1215, the ordeals ended, and it was the church that killed them. Theologians and canon lawyers argued that the ordeals were not true sacraments, and thus violated the biblical injunction against tempting God. And the ordeals were unknown in Roman law, which was increasingly revered. Critics also observed that there was potential for manipulation in the administration of the ordeals. In short, argued the churchmen, the ordeals were useless in determining a true judgment. And so, at the Fourth Lateran Council of 1215, the Church declared that henceforth no cleric could participate in an ordeal. Without a priest calling on God, the ordeal was dead.

Rulers all over Europe panicked. What now? What could possibly replace the judgment of God? The responses of rulers to these questions marked the great divide between the common-law legal system on the one hand and the civil-law or inquisitorial system on the other.

The church already had an answer. It had begun to develop, for its internal use, an alternative system of adjudication. The church had extensive needs for legal decision-making, both civil and criminal. It governed a vast personnel of priests, monks, and nuns who were exempt from criminal process in secular courts. It also held a large amount of land. The church needed some better way of finding facts and applying law to facts than ordeals and trial by combat.

The system that the church developed relied on investigation and adjudication by professional judges, with the option of a thorough appeal. This was the road that England did not take. But the rest of Western Europe did. By 1215 the church system of investigation and adjudication, also known as the Roman-canon system, was well developed and ready for adoption by secular rulers. A major requirement was a substantial body of literate, legally trained judges.

In criminal cases, the Roman-canon system ran into a difficulty. Rulers were terrified about giving up the judgment of God, and so they wanted to limit human discretion as much as possible. The way they did that was to require, in order to convict, one of two types of proof: the testimony of two unimpeachable eyewitnesses or a confession. Because for many crimes two unimpeachable eyewitnesses were not available, judges had to try to get a confession. Such a high bar for a conviction, such a supposed protection for the accused, led to coercion. Thus was born judicial torture. There were safeguards, such as threshold requirements of proof before torture began and corroboration of answers. But the potential for abuse is clear, as is the cruelty of the method, even used on a guilty defendant. Judicial torture became more limited starting in the sixteenth century, and it was almost entirely abolished in the eighteenth, as judges began deciding questions of fact without requiring a confession.

But in the minds of English lawyers and judges, the stain of judicial torture tainted the entire Roman-canon system. Common-law lawyers and judges equated jury trial with freedom from torture, and so did some Enlightenment thinkers on the continent of Europe.

Meanwhile, in England, the king faced a similar shock because of the abolition of the ordeals. The advisers to Henry II's grandson Henry III were clearly baffled. In 1219 the boy king issued a decree instructing the royal judges simply to hold those accused of serious crimes in prison. Essentially, the judges were being told it was up to them to figure out what to do.

What the judges began to do is understandable, in light of England's developing use of juries. Besides instituting the jury of accusation, Henry II had already instructed judges to use ordinary juries of twelve to decide certain civil cases. The judges applied this method to criminal cases. They gathered together twelve ordinary jurors and required them to give a verdict as to the accused's guilt. The jurors were expected to know about the question of guilt, just as they were expected to know who was suspected of a crime. In such a close-knit communal society, the jurors were supposed to be self-informing. Compared with ordeals, this jury trial was indeed a rational proceeding.

The use of unpaid lay jurors to decide cases conferred a great financial benefit on English kings; it saved them a lot of money. The institution allowed the English kings to get by with very few royal judges. The judges did not need to investigate facts, assemble evidence, or even adjudicate. Instead, the judges periodically rode around the English counties in pairs, collecting the presentments of juries of accusation and the verdicts of civil and criminal juries. In all of England at any given time there were only between twelve and fifteen royal judges. That number remained fixed into the late eighteenth century, at a time when the population of metropolitan London alone was more than one million. In contrast, the civil-law systems on the continent of Europe required hundreds and sometimes thousands of professional judges. And English judges gained an advantage from their small numbers. English judges' pay and prestige were high, compared with their counterparts on the continent.

A problem immediately arose. As the experience in continental Europe suggested, it was no small thing to go from the judgment of God to that of men. The royal judges thought that the legitimacy of a criminal jury depended on the consent of the accused. In other words, this method of adjudication had to be chosen by the defendant. It was, in effect, a form of arbitration.

But what if the accused did not consent to a jury decision? Then the judges were in a quandary. And so, like the legal systems on the continent of Europe, the English legal system resorted to

3. The pressing of William Spiggot in Newgate prison in London, 1721, is an example of *peine forte et dure*, literally hard and strong punishment. The common-law system used this procedure to coerce criminal defendants into accepting jury trial. With 400 pounds on his chest, Spiggot agreed to be tried by a jury. The leader of a gang of robbers, he was convicted and hanged days later.

coercion. The torture was called *peine forte et dure*, strong and hard punishment. An accused who refused to accept a jury was spread out on the ground and tied down, with a board on his chest. Weights were then piled on his chest until either he accepted trial by jury or was crushed to death.

Astonishingly, the English legal system continued this practice into the eighteenth century; legislation finally abolished it in 1772. It lasted so long because the procedure created a loophole. A defendant who was crushed to death was not convicted. This meant that his lands and personal property would pass to his heirs, rather than being confiscated by the Crown. For centuries, some propertied defendants wanted to take advantage of this loophole. A few instances of *peine forte et dure* even occurred in the American colonies. In 1692, 80-year-old Giles Corey was accused during the Salem witch trials in Massachusetts. Rather than stand trial, where he believed he was certain to be condemned as a warlock, Corey chose to be crushed to death so that his property could pass to his heirs.

Into the twentieth century, the English legal system maintained a vestige of the fiction that the defendant chose jury trial. Every felony defendant was asked, "How wilt thou be tried?" And the answer he was supposed to give was "By God and by my country." This meant trial by a jury, which represented both God and the entire people. Legislation of 1827 provided that, if he refused to answer, a plea of not guilty would be entered and jury trial would occur anyway.

The myth of Magna Carta and jury trial

In the history of the English jury, by far the most important event of 1215 was the Fourth Lateran Council in Rome, which abolished the ordeals. But another event occurred that year, one that has eclipsed the Fourth Lateran Council in the folklore of the jury. That event was the sealing of Magna Carta. Through interpretations centuries later, Magna Carta became associated with a right to ordinary jury trial. But, originally, Magna Carta was certainly not a guarantee of common-law jury trial. It could hardly have been; in 1215 criminal jury trial was not yet established. Later writers, though, claimed that Magna Carta enshrined juries as a check on royal power.

King John, the son of Henry II, had been exiling his political opponents, seizing their property, executing them, and making war on them—all without any legal judgment. The barons had had enough, and they rebelled against John. In June 1215, they cornered him in a marshy meadow near the Thames called Runnymede and forced him to agree to a list of sixty-one demands. These became known as the great charter, or Magna Carta. It purported to bind King John and his heirs "forever"; it claimed to be a sort of fundamental law.

Article 29 declared that the king could not exercise power against his subjects simply as he saw fit. He had to proceed by "the lawful judgment of his peers" or by "the law of the land." By "judgment of his peers," the barons did not mean ordinary jury trial, as it did not yet exist in criminal cases. In any event, the barons did not consider ordinary jurors to be their peers. They did not even consider royal judges to be their peers. They believed that they should be tried by each other. This idea was continued in the trial of peers in the House of Lords. (A fictional example, the trial of a duke for murder, occurs in Dorothy Sayers's 1926 mystery novel *Clouds of Witness*.)

But beginning in the sixteenth and seventeenth centuries, interpretations of Magna Carta equated "judgment of his peers" with ordinary jury trial. This link aided the quest to limit royal power. Against the assertions of royal absolutism by Stuart King Charles I, writers such as Sir Edward Coke cited Magna Carta and claimed a right to jury trial. The 1628 Petition of Right, which Coke helped to draft, quoted Magna Carta as stating that the king could not proceed against his subjects "but by the lawful judgment of his peers, or by the law of the land." In the Petition of Right, "judgment of his peers" was understood to mean trial by jury. Coke cemented this interpretation in his influential work *Second Institutes of the Laws of England*. Ever since, many have claimed that Magna Carta enshrined a right to jury trial. These included the American revolutionaries as well as the authors of almost every popular history of the jury.

The instructional trial

In the beginning, for the most part, medieval juries were expected to be self-informing. Some evidence could be presented in court. Still, "jury trial" was not yet a routine procedure. But a cataclysmic event changed that.

In October 1347, according to historian Barbara Tuchman, trading ships reached the harbor of Messina in Sicily "with dead and dying men at the oars." The ships had come from a Genoese trading post on the Black Sea. "The diseased sailors showed strange black swellings about the size of an egg or an apple in the armpits and groin. The swellings oozed blood and pus and were followed by spreading boils and black blotches on the skin from internal bleeding." The bubonic plague had arrived in Europe. In the summer of 1348, it reached England. Within several years, an estimated 40 percent of the population of Europe, including England, was dead.

The Black Death is not normally associated with a huge change in the English legal system. But that was its effect. The sudden chaos in society is hard to imagine. Whole villages were abandoned, and the survivors fled to other locales. The idea behind the creation of juries in the twelfth and thirteenth centuries was that juries were self-informing. The jurors were supposed to be able to tap into the deep local knowledge formed in tight-knit rural villages working in an open-field system. Now those conditions were gone. The growth of towns, with their larger and more transient populations, further depleted local knowledge. After the Black Death, jurors did not know their neighbors as they used to. They were less informed about events where they lived.

In time, evidence began to be routinely presented to the jury in court. The instructional jury trial had begun. What then was the rationale for the jury? With the advent of the instructional trial, the judge was hearing the same evidence as the jurors. Why not skip the jurors and have the judge make the decision?

English judges strongly favored the jury. In 1470, the English judge Sir John Fortescue wrote an account of the common-law system. In it, he emphasized the impartiality of the jurors. The jurors were, he wrote, of independent means (this was after the institution of property requirements), "sound in repute and fair-minded," not brought into court by either party, "but chosen by a respectable and impartial officer." The jurors were no longer being chosen for their knowledge of the case, but for their impartiality.

In this passage, Fortescue did not mention the point that the judge also had to be impartial. The trouble of calling together a jury might therefore have been spared. But English judges had powerful reasons for keeping the institution.

Chapter 2
Reasons for lay jurors in early modern and modern societies

One of the strongest reasons for using the jury, and one that still exists today in some places, is to solve the problem of judicial bias. Until the Glorious Revolution of 1688–9, English judges were suspect because they were not independent. Far from it; the judges were appointed by the Crown and served at the Crown's pleasure. In most ordinary cases, this lack of independence made little difference. But in political cases, the judges were aware that the eyes of the royal administration were on them.

The late Stuart kings did not hesitate to remove any judges whose decisions were not to their liking. Recall that at any given time in England, there were only about twelve judges, fifteen at most. During eight years of his reign, Charles II removed eleven judges. His brother, James II, outdid him, removing thirteen judges in four years.

The pressure on judges was especially intense in treason trials. High treason was plotting against the monarch's life, and the Crown took a great interest in these trials. In the sixteenth and seventeenth centuries, Crown lawyers prosecuted many people for conspiring against the monarch, culminating in a ferocious spate of trials in the late seventeenth century under the late Stuart kings. In these treason cases, the judges openly displayed hostility toward the defendant and permitted false and fabricated evidence.

The most notorious of the late Stuart judges were William Scroggs and George Jeffreys, whose names have become bywords for judicial bias. Chief Justice Scroggs is best known for presiding at a series of cases in 1678 called the Popish Plot trials. At one of these, a prosecution against Jesuit priests, Scroggs declared: "They eat their God, they kill their King, and saint the murderer!"

The late seventeenth-century treason cases resonated in common-law legal systems for centuries. They triggered a major series of defensive safeguards that locked in the adversarial system. In fact, many of the reforms—the rights to use counsel, to compel defense witnesses to attend court, and to confront opposing witnesses—are now enshrined in the first eight amendments of the U.S. Constitution.

Also enshrined in the U.S. Constitution, in Article III, is perhaps the most important reform: judicial independence. By the time the U.S. Constitution was drafted in 1787, judicial independence in England was nearly complete. Article III of the U.S. Constitution provided full independence for federal judges, with life tenure and salary protection.

The earlier judicial subservience to the Crown puts into context William Blackstone's extraordinary praise for the jury. Blackstone's foundational work, *Commentaries on the Laws of England*, published 1765–70, educated generations of common-law lawyers. Courts in the United States still regularly cite it as high authority, if not the highest authority, for the English common law of the period. In the *Commentaries*, Blackstone indulged in effusive rhetoric about the jury. One of the most quoted phrases in that much-quoted work is: "the trial by jury ever has been, and I trust ever will be, looked upon as the glory of the English law." Blackstone was attuned to the dangers of lack of judicial independence and judges' potential bias. Shortly after this famous passage, he gave reasons for his high opinion of juries. By far the most important reason was their role as a check on judicial partiality and bias.

The problem of the subservient bench also existed in the American colonies. Royal governors could dismiss colonial judges at will. No wonder that Article III of the U.S. Constitution protects judicial independence carefully. So carefully, in fact, that the Anti-Federalists, who opposed ratification of the Constitution, complained that the federal judiciary would be too independent and ultimately tyrannical. Federal judges, they argued, could be controlled by no other power. As the Anti-Federalist Brutus put it, federal judges "are independent of the people, of the legislature, and of every power under heaven. Men placed in this situation will generally soon feel themselves independent of heaven itself." The Anti-Federalists thought that juries were necessary to counteract this potential judicial tyranny. A right to criminal jury trial was already in the draft U.S. Constitution sent to the states for ratification. But the Anti-Federalists were deeply concerned about the lack of a guarantee of civil jury trial.

Alexander Hamilton, arguing in favor of ratification of the new constitution in New York, responded to these criticisms. In *The Federalist*, Hamilton addressed the judiciary and juries. He soothingly argued that the judiciary is "beyond comparison the weakest of the three branches of government," and plagued by "natural feebleness." He declared that judicial independence was necessary for judges to play their vital role of safeguarding liberties in a republic.

What about the jury? The jury could indeed play a role, Hamilton wrote, in protecting liberty and guarding against government and judicial overreach and bias. Both the Federalists and the Anti-Federalists agreed on that. "The friends and adversaries of the plan of the convention, if they agree in nothing else, concur at least in the value they set upon the trial by jury; or if there is any difference between them, it consists in this: the former regard it as a valuable safeguard to liberty, the latter represent it as the very palladium of free government." Here Hamilton was referring to the criminal jury.

Hamilton's view of the civil jury was more mixed. He argued against inclusion of a right to civil jury trial in the U.S. Constitution, on the grounds that such a right would be difficult to define and that the question of when to use civil juries was best left to the legislature. But Hamilton observed that the strongest argument in favor of the civil jury was that it could help to protect against judicial corruption.

Despite Hamilton's arguments, the Anti-Federalists were not reassured. Ratifying conventions in several states viewed the right to civil jury trial in federal courts as so important that they recommended its inclusion in an amendment to the Constitution, and in some cases almost succeeded in conditioning ratification on such a right.

James Madison tried to respond to these concerns in drafting what became the Seventh Amendment. In the Virginia ratifying convention, he had argued, against Patrick Henry, that there was no need for a civil jury right in the federal Constitution. But Madison was eager to avoid a second constitutional convention, which in his mind was a real possibility. And, to make assurance double-sure, he also included in his proposed amendments a right to criminal jury trial—even though that right already existed in the body of the Constitution.

The Anti-Federalists won their point. They got constitutional guarantees of jury trial to check the power of the federal judiciary. Whether juries have proved to be a sufficient check on the power of federal judges is another matter.

Among the judicial biases that juries could potentially check was class bias. In Blackstone's view, not only did juries protect against the general bias of the judge, the institution specifically counteracted class bias. Meanwhile, judges counteracted the capriciousness of juries:

The impartial administration of justice, which secures both our persons and our properties, is the great end of civil society. But if that be entirely entrusted to the magistracy, a select body of men, and those generally selected by the prince or such as enjoy the highest offices in the state, their decisions, in spite of their own natural integrity, will have frequently an involuntary bias towards those of their own rank and dignity: it is not to be expected from human nature, that *the few* should be always attentive to the interests and good of *the many*. On the other hand, if the power of judicature were placed at random in the hands of the multitude, their decisions would be wild and capricious, and a new rule of action would be every day established in our courts.

Concerns about judicial bias, including class bias, have encouraged the adoption of lay jurors in both South Korea in 2008 and Japan in 2009. Both of these are fundamentally civil-law systems, although both have adopted certain adversarial features. Japan had an earlier history of the use of criminal juries, from 1928 to 1943; criminal juries began during a period of expanding democracy, but their use declined dramatically as the country became more militaristic. Korea had no history of using lay jurors at all. In the early twenty-first century, the perceived problems with the judiciary in the two countries were similar, although the method of using lay jurors in each is quite different.

In both South Korea and Japan, supporters of lay jurors emphasized the need to bolster the popular legitimacy of criminal justice. But underlying this stated reason was concern about perceptions of the judiciary. In both countries, the judiciaries were perceived as elite and removed from the concerns of ordinary people. Many judges are graduates of prestigious universities, have earned top scores on difficult exams, come from affluent backgrounds, and are part of an insular judicial culture. More importantly for many citizens, judges in both countries are thought to be too lenient in dealing with elite defendants who were involved in corruption, and with defendants who had committed sex crimes. Sometimes these were the same. At the root of some of these problems are questions about judicial independence.

In South Korea, polls indicated that the public, and even more so lawyers, thought that sentences in general were too lenient. A particular focus of discontent was the light sentences of defendants who were connected with the "chaebols," the powerful corporate conglomerates that are still largely family-owned and controlled—for example, Daewoo and Samsung. It got to be a running and bitter joke with the public that a member of a chaebol family who was convicted, no matter what the crime, would receive a suspended sentence with no conditions. Essentially, the person would walk free. Judges could explain their decisions by pointing to mitigating factors, such as the defendant's employment and ability to make financial restitution to the victim. South Korean judges had, and still have, an incentive to give elite defendants light sentences because many of the judges go on to careers as practicing lawyers. Not surprisingly, the most lucrative clients are the chaebols.

There are also problems concerning judicial independence in Japan. The members of the Supreme Court and lower courts are appointed by the cabinet. Judges are therefore inclined to support the positions of the government, particularly as the same party, the Liberal Democratic Party, or LDP, has dominated elections almost continuously since its founding in 1955. Japanese judges pride themselves on not taking bribes or engaging in other sorts of corruption, but they are suspected of more subtle forms of bias. Citizens have complained that Japanese judges tended to give light sentences to high-ranking government officials and their friends and families, and also to corporate elites. Meanwhile, defense counsel have complained about rates of conviction by judges that top 99 percent, suggesting, in their view, excessive deference to the powerful Japanese police and to prosecutors.

To try to mitigate these concerns, both South Korea and Japan introduced lay juror participation into their criminal justice systems. In 2008, South Korea adopted an advisory jury invoked at the option of the defendant. A Korean judge is not bound by the opinion of the jury, but if the judge decides differently, the judge must explain why in writing.

In 2009, Japan reformed its citizen panels that review prosecutorial charges, and instituted a mixed panel for trial of a narrow range of cases. The mixed panel of three professional judges and six lay jurors is called the *saiban-in* system, meaning lay judge trial. The mixed panel decides both guilt and sentence.

While these reforms have had some effect, it is fair to say that the judges in both countries—and prosecutors in Japan—have succeeded in minimizing changes to the criminal justice system. In Korea, few defendants opt for a jury, as a major purpose of lay participation was to make sentences more severe. Making the jury available at the defendant's option was a choice that profoundly

4. The Japanese *saiban-in* system uses a mixed panel of three professional judges and six lay jurors. The three professional judges are in the center of the bench; the six lay jurors sit on either side of them.

discouraged popular input into the justice system. In 2018, only 180 Korean jury trials occurred. Korean judges are busy spending the money allocated for jury trials for other purposes.

In Japan, empirical research shows that the reforms of its citizen review panels have had little effect. Likewise, the results of the mixed panel have been limited. For the first years of the new system's operation, the mixed panels occasionally gave tougher sentences than the prosecution requested, especially in homicide cases. But the judges began to exert more control over sentencing by growing reference to a computerized database of sentences and thorough appellate review. Currently, mixed panels rarely deviate from the prosecutor's sentencing recommendation, except to award more suspended sentences in cases of robbery. Conviction rates by the mixed panels remain extremely high— over 99 percent, as in the previous era of judges' decisions. Part of the explanation may lie in the growing caution of prosecutors in charging cases. In any event, mixed panels through 2017 decided only a small number of criminal cases charged in Japan—about 1.5 percent. All other cases were decided by judges alone. Because of the narrow scope of mixed panel trials, mixed panels do not hear most cases of political corruption or rape. And those cases were the main impetus for reform in the first place.

At this point, both Japan's and Korea's introduction of lay jurors could aptly be characterized as window dressing. But this window dressing has to some extent been successful. In Japan, polls reveal fairly high levels of support for the lay juror system. It appears that this reform has, at least in part, achieved its goal of building popular legitimacy for the criminal justice system. No wonder that over 90 percent of Japanese judges have declared themselves in support of this method of using lay jurors.

In the United States today, the question of class bias on the part of judges remains salient. Certain issues or types of litigants raise the question. These include cases in which corporations are litigants, especially if the opposing party is an individual. Studies have consistently shown that juries, when compared with judges, strongly tend to favor individual litigants over corporations. The poorer and less educated a juror is, the more likely that juror is to oppose corporations. This difference between judges and juries might reflect not so much the bias of the judge as the bias of the juror.

Another area of persistent disagreement between judges and juries concerns firearms and self-defense. Judges, who in the United States are typically middle class at least, live lives that are relatively safe. Because of where they work (secure courthouses), live, shop, and so on, they can largely insulate themselves from criminal violence. And in the United States, any threats made against judges are taken seriously and sometimes trigger extra protection by guards. But other people are not so lucky. They do face criminal violence, some routinely. In general, juries tend to be more sympathetic to the claim of use of force in self-defense than judges. A salient example was the 1987 trial of a white man, Bernhard Goetz, for shooting four Black youths who allegedly tried to rob him on a New York subway. The jury acquitted Goetz of the most serious charges.

Class bias is not the only type of bias that might affect judges. In the United States, the elected judiciary poses special problems. Beginning in the mid-nineteenth century, many states started to elect judges. Currently over 80 percent of state judges face some type of election. Judicial campaigns often attract large contributions. These contributors expect to get something for their money, and they often do. The largest contributors to many judicial campaigns are the lawyers who are likely to appear before the judges, especially plaintiffs' lawyers. In the United States, plaintiffs' lawyers have a direct interest in the outcomes of cases because they are paid by contingent fee, that is, by a share of the recovery. This fee is usually at least one-third of the recovery. They therefore have a stronger incentive to contribute to judicial campaigns than defense lawyers, who are typically paid by the hour. But even defense lawyers have some incentive to contribute, to appear credible to their clients as having influence. Unions and corporations, the latter often through the U.S. Chamber of Commerce, also contribute large amounts to judicial campaigns. And the political parties contribute heavily.

The result is that elected judges may be biased, either subtly or not so subtly, toward their campaign contributors and against funders of their opponents. Elected judges also tend to favor litigants from their own districts, as these are their constituents and potential votes. Likewise, elected judges are biased against litigants from outside their districts, which often include large multistate or multinational corporations. In one Mississippi civil trial, the elected judge referred to the counsel for the defendant as "Mr. General Motors." In some parts of the country—notably southern Illinois and Louisiana—judges are so biased in favor of plaintiffs' lawyers and against defendant corporations that insurance defense lawyers strongly prefer the decision of a jury to that of a judge. They prefer juries despite the well-known hostility of juries to corporations generally, and especially insurance companies. In these areas, insurance defense lawyers always make what is called a jury demand. When asked why, defense lawyers smile and say, "Sure, juries hate insurance companies. But not as much as Judge X." There is therefore evidence that juries do in fact act as a check on the biases of an elected judiciary, especially in civil cases.

These problems of judicial bias are compounded where judges are scarce. In some counties in the United States, particularly in the Midwest and West, only a single judge sits. In the United States, many matters that trial judges decide are not subject to appellate review, or only to a limited extent. There is little check on this potential tyrant except for juries.

The jury as representative of the people

For many people today, one of the first rationales for the jury that springs to mind is that the institution makes judgments seem more legitimate to the people. The people are more attached to the justice system and more supportive of its decisions because they have a direct hand in making them. In many places, the jury has become a major symbol of the rule of the people—a sign of democracy itself, second only to voting in elections.

This rationale for the jury came late. We begin to glimpse it in the eighteenth century, and it resolves more clearly in the nineteenth century. The timing of its appearance and flourishing suggests that this rationale is closely linked to democracy and equality. It can be helpful for an aristocratic society to be attuned to popular legitimacy; in a democratic society, popular legitimacy is vital.

The most striking writer on this point was not English or American but French. The political philosopher Alexis de Tocqueville was eager to examine the first modern democracy. In his classic book *Democracy in America* (1835–40), Tocqueville aimed to reveal how democracy could be sustained and controlled. He believed that he found an important answer in judges and juries. Tocqueville did not repeat Anglo-American cheerleading slogans about the jury. He wrote that the jury could be considered as a judicial institution or as a political institution. The job of a judicial institution was to decide cases accurately and efficiently. As a judicial institution, Tocqueville strongly implied, the jury fell short.

But Tocqueville explained that "the jury is above all a political institution; it should be regarded as one form of the sovereignty of the people." Every citizen who could vote, Tocqueville insisted, should be able to serve on a jury. "Juries invest each citizen with a sort of magisterial office; they make all men feel that they have duties toward society and that they take a share in its government."

Democratic revolutionaries and liberal reformers the world over have shown their dedication to the cause by instituting juries. Sometimes this turn toward juries has been purely symbolic, and sometimes juries have actually begun operation. In almost all places, the revolutionaries and reformers urged jury trial in criminal cases, but not civil cases. Criminal prosecutions were thought to be the more dangerous exercise of state power, and easier for lay jurors to understand.

One of the earliest revolutionary countries to adopt jury trial, and one whose practice was influential throughout Europe and beyond, was France. French Enlightenment thinkers such as Montesquieu and Voltaire had praised the English institution of the jury. The jury, they believed, was key to the preservation of English liberty. During the first stages of the French Revolution, the delegates who met in the Constituent Assembly of 1789–91 agreed. The jury represented the transfer of sovereignty from the king to the people. The jury symbolized democracy itself.

The first modern jury trials in France occurred in March 1792, to wild popular acclaim. That enthusiasm diminished over time, as jurors were thought to be too confused by the law and evidence, and too lenient toward lawbreakers.

Nevertheless, the revolutionary French fervor for juries caught on throughout Europe and elsewhere in the world, at least as a symbol of democracy. Many of the German states, following the liberal revolutions of 1848, hastened to gain popular legitimacy and appease democratic sentiment by adopting jury trial. The U.S. Constitution has also been an influence, especially in Latin America. Some countries have tended toward the symbolic praise of juries and have taken a long time to put juries into practice. A constitutional guarantee of jury trial has proved to be no guarantee of actual juries. The liberal Spanish constitutions of 1812, 1837, and 1869 all provided for jury trial, but there was no legislation and actual use of juries until 1888. Those juries ended in the 1930s as the Spanish civil war began. The post-Franco constitution of 1978 provided for lay participation in trials, but the opposition of Spanish judges prevented use of juries until a law of 1995. Likewise, the Argentine constitution of 1858 called for jury trials, but the provision was not implemented. Finally, after decades of bloody military dictatorships, in 2011 some Argentine provinces, including Buenos Aires, began jury trial in criminal cases.

On the other hand, some countries in Latin America actually implemented jury trial soon after declaring it a right. These include Mexico in its constitution of 1824, swiftly following independence from Spain, and Brazil when it became independent from Portugal in 1822. Brazil has continued its use of juries. In Mexico, the liberal dream of jury trial faded. Beginning in the 1830s, a power struggle between oligarchic families, the Catholic church, and the military, none of whom wanted juries, undermined jury trial. Liberal reformers such as José María Luis Mora argued vigorously for the continuance of the jury, and Mexico maintained some form of jury trial into the twentieth century. But following the rise of the National Revolutionary Party in 1929, jury trials dwindled almost to vanishing. In 2008, major Mexican reforms of criminal procedure did not revive jury trial, but rather rely on combinations of judges to check corruption.

Russia's experience illustrates how the use of jury trial tracks the rise, fall, and revival of liberal, pro-democratic sentiments. During a liberalizing period, Tsar Alexander II's judicial reforms of 1864 instituted jury trials in Russia. In 1917, the Bolsheviks abolished juries. Following the fall of the communist Soviet regime, Russia reinstated jury trial in 1993. The former Soviet republics continue to turn to jury trial as a symbol of democratic legitimacy.

Like colonial Americans, Indians under British rule clung to native juries as an element of popular participation in government. This was especially true of Indian elites. In 1892, the government of Calcutta (now Kolkata) reduced the use of jury trial by executive order. As American colonists did earlier, Bengali leaders protested that curtailing jury trial would "disturb the trust of the people in the Government" and "take away one of the greatest safeguards of liberty." During the 1890s throughout India, native political parties called for an extension of jury trial to further Indians' participation in government and to prepare the way for home rule.

The jury as a school for democracy

With the advent of modern democracy, a problem arose. How could so many persons be able to make wise decisions, or at least wise enough to keep liberty and self-government going? When Tocqueville read works by American authors and talked with American lawyers and judges, he picked up the idea of the jury as a school for democracy. Some Americans are so familiar with this idea that we fail to recognize how novel it was. The jurors were not a means to an end; they were the end. The institution existed for them. Tocqueville declared that the jury was "a free school" for democracy. "I do not know whether a jury is useful to the litigants, but I am sure it is very good for those who have to decide the case. I regard it as one of the most effective means of popular education at society's disposal."

How was this education of jurors accomplished? Tocqueville had no use for the argument often made today that what educates jurors is the act of deliberating with fellow jurors. According to this idea, jurors who deliberate together learn to listen to each other, to hear different points of view, and to continue to reason together to achieve a mutually agreeable outcome. Jury service therefore contributes to deliberative democracy. Proponents of this argument downplay the possibility that jurors might refuse to listen to each other, or be appalled at the incompetence and misguidedness of their fellows, or crudely compromise, or follow the leader. Tocqueville did not mention jurors learning from deliberations at all. Indeed, his discussion suggests that, without firm guidance from the judge, jury deliberations would be the blind leading the blind.

In Tocqueville's view, the key mechanisms for juror education were not deliberations, but rather the juror's task of deciding a case and the judge's powerful guidance. Tocqueville thought that in civil cases particularly, the judge provided that element of impartial, intelligent authority—an "aristocratic body"—without which democracy might descend into chaos. In civil cases, jurors would often be at a loss without the judge; "the judge appears as a disinterested arbitrator between the litigants' passions." The jurors "feel confidence in him and listen to him with respect, for here his intelligence completely dominates theirs." The judge cleared up confusion caused by testimony and by the arguments of counsel: "It is he who unravels the various arguments they are finding it so hard to remember and takes them by the hand to guide them through procedural intricacies; it is he who limits their task to the question of fact and tells them what answer to give on questions of law." The result was that the jurors rendered the decision made by the judge. "He has almost unlimited power over them."

In other words, according to Tocqueville, a large part of the jurors' education was to learn to defer to a more competent authority. Commentators on Tocqueville seldom mention, or perhaps notice, this point.

For Americans, Tocqueville's description of the judge dominating a civil jury is surprising, to say the least. That is not what happens today, and it was not what happened in many American courtrooms at the time Tocqueville was writing. Tocqueville exaggerated the power of the American judge, and he downplayed the power of the lawyers. In fact, Tocqueville's account was much more accurate as a description of what happened in English courtrooms. English judges had great powers to comment on the evidence and to guide the jury, powers that many American judges lacked.

No matter. American commentators and judges conveniently lopped off Tocqueville's bold assertions about judicial power and the importance of jurors deferring to judges' authority. Many of them also suppressed Tocqueville's doubts about the jury as a judicial institution. After purging such uncomfortable points, American writers have happily followed Tocqueville in calling the jury a "free school" for democracy. Some claim that this is the main benefit of the jury.

That benefit appears to be small. In the first place, the number of persons who serve on juries is dwindling, as rates of plea bargaining in criminal cases and settlement rates in civil cases soar. Persons who do not serve on juries cannot be educated by the experience. In a 2012 survey of U.S. adults, 27 percent reported that they had served on a jury at some point in their lives. In 2007, the National Center for State Courts estimated that, in any given year, 1.5 million Americans serve on a jury in state court, less than one percent of the adult U.S. population. The numbers of federal jurors are much smaller, about 54,000 in 2016.

Second, studies have detected only a limited relationship between service on a jury and greater civic engagement. Empirical work suggests that service as a juror promotes political participation. But the effects are modest and limited to those who were not politically active before. For jurors with "a relatively spotty voting record," a nationwide study found an average voter turnout increase of 4 to 7 percent. For jurors who were already active voters, there was no change in voting behavior. Jurors who were the most active participants in deliberations showed a small-to-moderate increase in participating in local community groups. If civic education is the main benefit of the jury, it appears to be

a small effect for an institution that has enormous consequences
for the legal system.

Most former jurors report that their experience was positive—
81 percent in a 2012 survey. Jurors usually believe that the
judge, court personnel, and the lawyers have treated them well.
A detailed survey of jurors in King County, Washington, which
includes the city of Seattle, reported that many jurors were
impressed with the importance of their job and the respectfulness
of deliberations. As one former juror put it, "the jury members,
although from different backgrounds, mindsets, etc., were very
considerate of others' feelings and fair in their dealings in
deliberating to change others' opinions." Others reported different
experiences. One juror said that another juror, on entering the
deliberation room, "when she sat down, turned her back to all of
us and faced the wall." This distressed and frustrated the other
jurors, causing one to burst into tears while driving home after the
first day of deliberations. It emerged that the back-turning juror
was holding out for a verdict of second-degree murder, whereas
the other jurors became convinced that the defendant was guilty
of premeditated murder in the first degree. The next day, the
back-turning juror got up and left the room for good; the judge
replaced her with an alternate. The jury then returned a verdict
of murder in the first degree. A juror in a different case said that
"during deliberations, we had a pig-headed juror who refused to
listen to reason or see the obvious, so we couldn't convict on
certain counts...this left me and several of the other jurors
very frustrated."

Sparing judges responsibility and criticism

We now come to a rationale for the jury that common-law judges
almost never state explicitly. But it is very much in their minds,
either in the foreground or in the background. Common-law
judges typically heap praise on the jury system. Even when they
acknowledge the errors that jurors make, judges still cling to the

jury. This is not entirely because of modern democratic tastes. We have seen the fifteenth-century judge Sir John Fortescue praise the jury, as well as the eighteenth-century writer (and later judge) Sir William Blackstone. The eminent seventeenth-century judge and legal writer Sir Matthew Hale agreed. None of these writers could be accused of a mindset of democratic equality.

Why then do common-law judges cleave to the jury so devotedly? As the French Enlightenment thinker Montesquieu pointed out, the power of judging is "terrible among men." It is greatly feared. Montesquieu knew this well, as he was a prominent judge on a French criminal court. As a French judge, he had no jury to hide behind. Judging in criminal cases, especially, is apt to attract resentment and criticism. This was a major reason why Montesquieu recommended, in his 1748 work *Spirit of the Laws*, that judging be done by lay jurors. In this way, he wrote, the power of judging "becomes, so to speak, invisible and null."

Use of lay juries deflects attention from the judges. Judges can claim that they had no responsibility for the outcome—it was the work of the people themselves. The lay jurors do the dirty work of deciding the facts and pronouncing the verdict, not the judge. The jurors get the responsibility and thus the blame. But they melt back into the body of the people and thus do not shoulder these burdens for long. Moreover, jurors may help to conceal the enormous role that common-law judges play in developing the law.

Only rarely is a judge capable of discussing this subject with candor. But there have been a few, and these have been among the most eminent. In the 1530s, Sir Thomas More, Lord Chancellor of England, said that the common-law judges "see that they may, by the verdict of the jury, cast off all quarrels from themselves upon them, which they account their chief defense." More also wrote that the judges refrained from deciding cases themselves, without a jury, "for the avoiding of obloquy." But, More declared, he would rather trust one judge than two juries. In the 1670s, Chief Justice

Sir Matthew Hale wrote, "It were the most unhappy case that could be to the judge, if he at his peril must take upon him the guilt or innocence of the prisoner."

Another striking proponent of the jury was Sir James Fitzjames Stephen, a late nineteenth-century English judge and criminologist. Stephen was quite open in describing the drawbacks of ordinary jurors, including being biased, misunderstanding law and evidence, and following a strong but mistaken leader. And yet he claimed that the jury was valuable. Stephen broached the topic of the jury sparing judges with some hesitation. He admitted that he was, "as every judge must be, a prejudiced witness on the subject." After these warnings, he gave a confession.

> It is hardly necessary to say that to judges in general the maintenance of trial by jury is of more importance than to any other members of the community. It saves judges from the responsibility—which to many men would appear intolerably heavy and painful—of deciding simply on their own opinion upon the guilt or innocence of the prisoner....
>
> [T]he institution of trial by jury is so very pleasant to judges that they may probably be prejudiced in its favor.

The jury was more important to judges, Stephen wrote, than to any other members of the community. That would include the public, lawyers, jurors themselves, victims, and criminal defendants. The nominally independent decision of the jury spared the judge both the internal pressure of making the decision entirely himself, and the external criticism that that decision might attract. Montesquieu, More, Hale, and Stephen all agreed that juries deflected attention and responsibility from judges. And most likely so have many other judges, whether or not they admit it.

Judges are not the only legal professionals who can use the decisions of juries to deflect responsibility and blame. In several high-profile cases of police use of force, prosecutors' use of grand juries performed the same function for them. The grand jury is the descendant of the jury of presentment that King Henry II established in the Middle Ages. The grand jury's main role is to decide whether to approve or to decline a prosecutor's charges against a defendant. Although England abolished the grand jury in 1948, about half the American states and the federal courts continue to require a grand jury to approve felony charges before a prosecution can proceed. The Fifth Amendment to the U.S. Constitution gives defendants a right to a grand jury, but that clause has not been applied to the states. A charge that a grand jury approves is called an indictment. Federal grand juries consist of between sixteen and twenty-three people; twelve votes are needed to indict. Typically, the prosecutor dominates the grand jury, as the prosecutor controls what evidence is presented to it; an old joke is that "a grand jury would indict a ham sandwich." But with politically fraught charges, the grand jury may be more than a rubber stamp. The decisions of grand juries declining charges against the white police officers who killed the Black Americans Michael Brown in Ferguson, Missouri, in 2014 and Breonna Taylor in Louisville, Kentucky, in 2020 have been controversial. But the prosecutors in those cases could say that those were decisions made by the people, not the prosecutors alone. In the Breonna Taylor case, one grand juror was distressed at being used as cover for the prosecutor: "Using the grand jurors as a shield to deflect accountability and responsibility for these decisions only sows more seeds of doubt in the process while leaving a cold chill down the spines of future grand jurors."

The jury as a benefit to lawyers

Just as judges are loud in their praise of the jury system, American lawyers are too. This is for good reason: the institution serves the interests of lawyers in important ways. One of these ways is that juries are an ideal audience for lawyers' rhetoric. Jurors are supposed to be paying attention; their decision matters. They are laypersons, and their lack of technical training makes them sensitive to emotional appeal. And they are a substantial group, not just one or a few individuals. These are dramatic conditions, in which lawyers' rhetoric can have a heightened impact—both on the jurors and on courtroom spectators. This display of rhetorical skill mattered much more in the nineteenth century, when jury trials were common, and many practicing lawyers had political ambitions. Dramatic courtroom advocacy was a powerful way for a lawyer to make a name for himself. The most famous lawyers regularly made jurors weep, and people flocked to the courthouse from miles around to hear them.

Later, too, often juries were an afterthought, and the spotlight was on the lawyers. Many movies featuring jury trials are much more about a heroic lawyer than the jurors; the 1959 drama *Anatomy of a Murder* and the 2001 comedy *Legally Blonde* are two of many such films. Movies that focus on the jurors, like the 1957 drama *12 Angry Men*, are much rarer.

With so few jury trials today, the jury's role as an audience for lawyers' rhetoric and the display of lawyers' trial skills is much diminished. Yet the civil jury still plays a vital role for American lawyers. This is because it confers a great financial benefit. Mainly through the tort system, the existence of juries transfers large amounts of wealth to lawyers, through plaintiffs' lawyers' contingent fees and defense lawyers' billing by the hour. For the decade 2000–10, the total cost of the U.S. tort system averaged $241.4 billion per year, of which 24.3 percent was administrative expense—including legal fees—for an average of $58.7 billion per year. And this transfer occurs despite the scarcity of jury trials. The vast majority of cases end by a settlement, or agreement between the parties. Bargaining for settlement of a case takes place "in the shadow of the jury," that is, based at least partly on a guess about what a jury would do in the case.

Studies have shown that the greatest area of disagreement between judges and juries concerns damages. In many parts of the country, juries award significantly higher damages than judges do. Jurors are apt to sympathize with injured local plaintiffs, especially individuals. Lawyers are well aware of the difference a jury makes to outcomes in cases, or at least the threat of a jury. And lawyers like their contingent fees and billable hours, which would be harder to charge in a simpler and more certain system of compensation.

This is the reason why trial lawyers fight tenaciously to retain civil jury trial and to ward off or limit administrative schemes of compensation for injuries, such as workers' compensation. For many years the American Bar Association has opposed administrative schemes for no-fault auto accident compensation. Today, it sponsors the Commission on the American Jury, dedicated to preserving and improving jury trial. An early warrior in the fight against no-fault auto accident compensation schemes was the flamboyant San Francisco trial lawyer Melvin Belli— known as "the king of torts." Belli was one of the founders of the organization of plaintiffs' lawyers that became known as the American Trial Lawyers Association (ATLA), now known as the American Association for Justice. Belli's 1950s and 1960s campaign against administrative compensation schemes played on Cold War themes that associated the common law and juries with liberty, and regulation with communism.

Although he fought for the right to jury trial, actual juries and trials were not necessary to achieve the outcomes Belli wanted. He understood the importance to the plaintiffs' bar of quick and generous settlements. To facilitate these, he energetically collected reports of jury verdicts and settlements and created tables of expected litigation outcomes that, ironically, resemble workers' compensation tables. He titled the first of his path-breaking articles on the subject "The Adequate Award." That was also the name he gave his 105-foot yacht.

Chapter 3
Jury power to nullify the law

Once the instructional trial began in the later Middles Ages and the judge and the jury were hearing the same evidence, disagreements between them could arise. Sometimes, the jury might willfully ignore the facts or the law. This became known as "jury nullification."

Jury nullification lives in many people's minds as pictures of heroic juries standing up to oppressive governments and vindicating the liberties of the people. And sometimes it was that. For that reason, the American founders insisted on jury trial. Even today, jury nullification can soften the application of harsh laws. As the eminent American judge Learned Hand observed, the institution of trial by jury necessarily "introduces a slack into the enforcement of the law, tempering its rigor by the mollifying influence of current ethical conventions." But nullification also has a darker side.

After the advent of the instructional trial, a division of labor arose between the judge and the jury. The judge was supposed to declare to the jury the relevant law, and the jurors were supposed to take the law as given them by the judge, without second-guessing it, and apply it to the facts as they found them. It was not always easy to separate a question of law for the judge from a question of fact for the jury. But that was and is the rule.

One difficulty is that sometimes the jury does not want to apply the law as given by the judge. And, at least if it acquits, the jury has the power not to. Because of the double jeopardy rule, the defendant cannot be tried twice for the same crime if the defendant is acquitted. The reason for the double jeopardy rule was to protect the defendant from abusive, multiple prosecutions for the same crime. Therefore the acquittal of a jury is final. The traditional common-law rule is that the prosecution cannot appeal. There is no mechanism for correcting an acquittal made in error. The jury thus has the power to acquit despite the law and the evidence.

Judges and juries were especially apt to disagree in cases involving laws about religious conformity and seditious libel, questions that implicate what we call today "free exercise of religion" and "free speech." Under modern liberal political theory, protecting these kinds of liberties is at the core of the aims of government. In the seventeenth century and into the eighteenth, these substantive rights were not protected. In these types of cases, English juries sometimes nullified the law.

In 1670 an English jury acquitted William Penn, the founder of Pennsylvania, and William Mead of charges of participating in a Quaker assembly, which an act of Parliament made illegal. There could be no doubt of Penn and Mead's guilt; in London, the pair openly preached Quakerism.

From a political standpoint, the reaction of English judges to this kind of jury nullification was brilliant. English judges decided to maintain and even enhance the power of juries. That way, judges could quietly promote liberty, if they chose, and, in any event, avoid political trouble.

The seminal decision was the opinion of John Vaughan, Chief Justice of Common Pleas, in 1670 in *Bushell's Case*. *Bushell's Case* stemmed directly from the case against Penn and Mead. After the jury acquitted Penn and Mead "contrary to the full and manifest evidence," as the trial judge put it, and against his instructions, the judge fined the jurors. Eight of the twelve jurors refused to pay the fine and were imprisoned. These jurors, including Edward Bushell, challenged the legality of their imprisonment in the Court of Common Pleas. Chief Justice Vaughan gave an opinion declaring that jurors could not be fined for disobeying the trial judge's instructions. The opinion obscured the real reason for refusing to fine and imprison jurors: to allow jury nullification.

Disingenuous as the opinion in *Bushell's Case* may have been, Vaughan achieved his goal of giving nominal independence to jurors. He therefore got English judges out of the politically charged business of making individual determinations on liberties. Judges could claim that if juries wanted to nullify the law in certain cases, that was the jurors' business and not the judges' fault. Rather than outright declaring substantive liberties, the English left these rights to a procedural mechanism, the jury.

Like Magna Carta, *Bushell's Case* lives in the modern folklore of the jury. In the United States, the Fully Informed Jury Association, a group dedicated to promoting jury nullification, has declared September 5 to be "Jury Rights Day" because it is the anniversary of William Penn's arrest.

Another substantive freedom that jury nullification sometimes protected was freedom of the press. English judges and juries battled over the issue in the form of prosecutions for seditious libel. Seditious libel was any written criticism of the government or government officials, even if true. In the American colonies, juries were even more reluctant to convict in seditious libel cases. Grand juries also refused to indict. Because of such nullification, the law of seditious libel became in effect a dead letter. The most famous example was the case of John Peter Zenger in 1735. The case reverberated through the centuries in the American story of the jury. In 1776, Gouverneur Morris, who was prominent in New York and Pennsylvania politics and an early advocate of American independence, claimed that the "trial of Zenger in 1735 was the germ of American Freedom—the morning star of that liberty which subsequently revolutionized America."

In the 1730s, the powerful Morris family—from which Gouverneur Morris was descended—funded a newspaper called the *New-York Weekly Journal* to oppose the policies of their political enemy, New York Governor William Cosby. John Peter Zenger was the printer of the paper. The editor of the paper, James Alexander, alternated attacks on Governor Cosby, in the form of anonymous letters to the editor, with articles praising freedom of the press. Cosby was determined to shut the paper down. The Chief Justice, James De Lancey, tried to persuade three different grand juries to indict Zenger for seditious libel, but all three refused. Finally, the attorney general of the colony filed an information—a charge made by a prosecutor alone, without a grand jury—against Zenger.

At trial, De Lancey insisted that the jurors find a special verdict, simply deciding whether Zenger published the words at issue. Then, he said, he would decide whether the words were a libel. Zenger's lawyer argued openly to the jurors that the jury should give a general verdict on the whole charge, and added that the words must be false to be a libel. Under the law at the time, both of those arguments were wrong. Nevertheless, the jury brought in a general verdict finding Zenger not guilty. According to the narrative later written by James Alexander and printed by Zenger, when the foreman announced the verdict, "there were three huzzas in the hall, which was crowded with people."

Nullifying laws restricting the press has historically been a significant function of the jury in different countries. In France during the supposedly liberal July Monarchy (1830–48), popular juries acquitted at high rates defendants charged with violating the new laws restricting the press—at a rate of 72 percent, according to one study. After Louis-Napoléon Bonaparte seized control of France in 1851, his dictatorial Second Empire regime quickly removed press cases from jury trial. In France, battles over the jurisdiction of juries in cases involving the press continued through the nineteenth century. Tsarist Russia also curtailed the use of juries in press and political cases, following jury nullification there. Similarly, in many German states after the 1848 revolutions, juries were no longer permitted to decide such cases. In all of the places that limited jury trial for press cases, an important substantive right—freedom of the press—did not exist. Jury nullification was the only remedy.

Besides seditious libel cases, which were criminal, American colonial juries also nullified the law in civil cases. As tensions with the British government grew, jury nullification became ever more prominent as a means of voiding hated British laws, especially customs taxes. In the 1761 case of *Erving v. Cradock*, for example, a Massachusetts merchant sued a customs inspector, who had caught the merchant smuggling, for trespass. He won a large verdict from a civil jury.

Parliament realized that jury nullification in the colonies threatened British rule, and it worked to curb colonial juries. In a series of acts including the Stamp Act of 1765, Parliament expanded the jurisdiction of the juryless admiralty courts, in an effort to prevent nullification of customs laws.

American colonists reacted by vigorously petitioning the British government for jury rights. In response to the Stamp Act, delegates from nine of the thirteen colonies met in New York the same year, a meeting known as the Stamp Act Congress. They adopted a Declaration of Rights and Grievances, which stated "[t]hat trial by jury is the inherent and invaluable right of every British subject in these colonies. . . . [The Stamp Act] and other acts, by extending the jurisdiction of the courts of admiralty beyond its ancient limits, have a manifest tendency to subvert the rights and liberties of the colonists." The Declaration of Independence of 1776 listed as a reason for separation from

Britain: "For depriving us, in many cases, of the benefits of trial by jury."

The history of juries nullifying unpopular British laws led the founders of the new republic to support broad powers for juries. At various times, John Adams, Thomas Jefferson, and even John Jay, when he became Chief Justice of the U.S. Supreme Court, declared that juries could decide the law, against the direction of the court. For Americans of the revolutionary generation, juries had served as a sort of mini-legislature at a time when the colonists had no representation in Parliament. On the Indian subcontinent in the late nineteenth and early twentieth centuries, a similar concern motivated some supporters of the Indian independence movement to argue in favor of juries.

With this background, the new states that wrote declarations of rights or constitutions hastened to provide the right to jury trial in both criminal and civil cases. Soon afterward, state civil juries began nullifying the law, particularly in favor of debtors and against foreigners. Protection of debtors through jury nullification was one of the reasons Anti-Federalists such as Patrick Henry argued so strongly for specifying a right to civil jury trial in the U.S. Constitution. But, in the ratification debates, Henry stopped short of openly calling for jury nullification. Why?

Once Americans moved to a republican form of government, jury nullification became deeply problematic. The situation was different from the colonial era. The people now had a say in the making of laws; they elected the representatives that made them. Why should twelve citizens have the power to nullify laws enacted by a legislature elected by the people? Furthermore, legislatures followed a process for enacting laws carefully specified in a written constitution, itself ratified by the people.

Revolutionaries favor juries deciding law, but once the revolution succeeds and a new government must be formed, it becomes a different matter. In comparing the American Revolution with the English revolution of 1688, historian Horace Gray observed: "The great constitutional lawyers and judges of either revolutionary period...with one voice maintained the right of the jury upon the general issue to judge of the law as well as the fact. But they had hardly passed away...when the courts of the new government began to assert as much control over the consciences of the jury, as had been claimed by the most arbitrary judges of the monarch whom that revolution had overthrown."

The desirability of jury nullification is a perennial debate, both among legal professionals and among citizens. Over time, the salient issues have changed. In the 1850s, especially in Massachusetts, opposition to the federal Fugitive Slave Act of 1850 generated new interest in jury nullification. New England juries refused to convict defendants accused of harboring fugitive slaves or aiding their escape. (Those fleeing slavery were not themselves entitled to jury trial.) This refusal set up a battle with judges, some of whom opposed slavery but believed that they must uphold the law. Judges were especially concerned that nullification in these cases would inflame tensions between the North and South.

After the Civil War, nullification became prominent again. Railroads drew jurors' special ire. The new railroads provided great benefits; their cheap and fast transport made the industrial revolution possible. But those benefits came at a cost. Railroads caused injuries of many sorts: livestock were struck and killed by trains; sparks flying from the wheels and smokestacks set crops on fire; and employees, passengers, and passers-by were injured and killed in the frequent accidents. Besides causing physical injury, railroads also charged monopoly prices and bribed legislators. Populist sentiment against railroads was widespread, and it became a potent political force.

Jurors were apt to disregard the law in favor of plaintiffs injured by railroads. An opinion by an English court in 1857, in a case for personal injury caused by the plaintiff falling down stairs on a railway platform, summed up the problem: "every person who has had any experience in courts of justice knows very well that a case of this sort against a railway company could only be submitted to a jury with one result."

In criminal cases during the late nineteenth century, courts firmly declared that the jury had a duty to follow the law as given by the judge. Because of the double jeopardy rule, the jury has the power to nullify the law by declaring the defendant not guilty. But judges announced that the jury's duty was to follow the law as given by the judge. The most prominent case was the U.S. Supreme Court's 1895 decision in *Sparf and Hansen v. United States*. Sparf and Hansen were sailors charged with the murder of the second mate of their ship on the high seas. A juror asked the judge whether the defendants would get capital punishment after a verdict of guilty, and the judge responded yes. (That was the penalty under the statute.) The juror then asked if there was anything else the jury could convict the defendants of—presumably, a crime that would not require capital punishment. The judge refused to give a different instruction, on the grounds that there was no evidence to justify it. The jury convicted the defendants of murder. The U.S. Supreme Court upheld the trial judge's decision, declaring that if nullification were encouraged, "our government will cease to be a government of laws, and become a government of men."

Despite judges' stern admonitions, nullification to protect particular substantive liberties continues. Jurors in Alaska are known for refusing to find defendants guilty of the federal crime of being a convicted felon in possession of a firearm. Many Alaskans appear to believe that firearms are necessary to survive there, in a state full of large and potentially dangerous wild animals. The Fully Informed Jury Association, a group that encourages jury nullification, seems to be particularly concerned about laws involving taxes, firearms, and drugs.

Nullification based on race, ethnicity, and religion

Although the jury's ability to nullify the law has been much celebrated, with many references to Zenger, nullification can be disturbing. In the United States, nullification has sometimes been based on the race of the defendant, at times in combination with the race of the victim.

During the twentieth century, white jurors in the South convicted Black defendants accused of crimes against whites on scanty evidence. A striking example was the conviction of eight young Black defendants of the rape of two white women in Scottsboro, Alabama, in 1931. Southern juries also refused to convict whites accused of murdering Black people, despite strong or overwhelming evidence. In 1964, there were hung juries in two trials of Byron De La Beckwith in Mississippi for the murder of NAACP field secretary Medgar Evers. In 1955, an all-white jury in Mississippi acquitted J. W. Milam and Roy Bryant of the murder of 14-year-old Emmett Till. Till's murder occurred because of his conversation with a white woman in her family's store. Protected by the double jeopardy rule, Milam and Bryant admitted in a 1956 interview with *Look* magazine that they had killed Till.

Race-based nullification continues. Today, jurors from the South Bronx in New York City are often reluctant to convict young Black men of crimes. After the 1990 acquittal in Washington, DC, of a defendant on first degree murder charges despite overwhelming evidence, a letter purporting to be from a juror stated that some jurors "didn't want to send any more Young Black Men to jail." As Professor Randall Kennedy of Harvard Law School pointed out, the victims of such defendants are mostly Black. Professor Kennedy described race-based nullification as a "sabotage of justice."

Chapter 4
Who serves as a juror?

The question of who serves as a juror is closely linked to the purpose of the jury. Is the primary purpose of the jury to be an impartial decision-maker, to be an expert decision-maker, to represent the entire community in giving judgment, or to maximize the power and wealth of lawyers? The answer to the question of purpose is key to determining the jury pool to be summoned and the process for choosing the jurors.

Many of these purposes are mutually incompatible—a problem not widely recognized today. For example, if the purpose of the jury is to be impartial, then the jury almost certainly will not be representative of the entire community. Certain biases and prejudices are widespread in any community, and they are often relevant to litigation. Jurors who have them, and are likely to act on them, will need to be eliminated in order for the jury to be impartial. Hard choices and tradeoffs are necessary.

In England, one of the earliest formal rules about who served on a jury had to do with making sure that the jury could be self-informing. To enable jurors to know about the case in advance, they were supposed to be from the locality where the events occurred—the "vicinage," or the hundred, the administrative unit containing about a hundred lawful men. Gradually, over the course of centuries, the requirement of being from the hundred was limited to ever-smaller numbers of jurors on the panel. The requirement dwindled because of the difficulty of getting enough jurors to serve and because of the advent of instructional trial, which meant that jurors no longer needed to be self-informing. Legislation in 1705 finally eliminated the requirement completely; jurors simply had to be from the county where events had occurred.

As the rationale for the jury shifted from bringing local knowledge to being impartial, other qualifications developed to try to achieve that goal. Jurors were not supposed to be related to the parties or to have an interest in the outcome of the case. Bribery of jurors was an early and persistent problem. A series of statutes beginning in the thirteenth century tried to curb bribery by requiring jurors to meet certain property qualifications. By the eighteenth century, service on juries in most courts required ownership of land, called a freehold, that produced at least £10 of income a year. The property requirement excluded two-thirds to three-quarters of adult men. Trial jurors were mostly from what was called "the middling sort"—yeoman farmers and merchants. Meanwhile, grand jurors had moved far up the social scale, and were typically upper-class. The gentry liked to control criminal charges.

In England, the property qualification for ordinary jurors persisted until 1972. Although by the twentieth century inflation had softened the requirements, still the rules excluded much of the working class—who rented rather than owned their homes—many women, and the young. As the prominent English judge Patrick Devlin put it in 1966, English juries were "predominantly male, middle-aged, middle-minded, and middle-class." The middle-mindedness was because professionals, such as lawyers and doctors, were automatically exempt from jury service. Such homogenous juries could often reach consensus and unanimous verdicts relatively quickly. But they were not representative of the population.

The United States inherited this tradition of property qualifications for jurors. In the eighteenth and nineteenth centuries, American legislation often required that jurors be "freeholders or householders." New York State required that a juror own land or personal property worth at least $250. But the dispersed population and the scarcity of jurors in many areas often meant that property qualifications were downplayed or ignored. Beginning in the nineteenth century, in uncoordinated fashion, the states eliminated these requirements by statute. New York and Texas were two of the last states to do so, eliminating their property requirements only in 1967 and 1969, respectively.

Many states have also reduced or eliminated exemptions from jury service, including New York's dramatic abolition of all exemptions in 1995. In 1999, then-Mayor Rudolph Giuliani served as a juror in a civil case. He was the only person in the jury box wearing a suit and tie.

When many European countries adopted juries in the nineteenth century, they instituted property qualifications. As in England, the requirements were intended both to prevent bribery and to ensure more educated jurors.

In France, the question of property qualifications for jurors was contentious, and policy swung wildly. Napoleon expressed strong views about property qualifications for jurors. The government of the Directory, which came into power following the overthrow of the Jacobins in 1794, had struggled to maintain order. Gangs of brigands freely roamed the French countryside. To the consternation of judges and the government, jurors frequently acquitted notorious criminals. When Napoleon took power in 1799, one of his top priorities was to restore law and order. An effective administrator as well as a brilliant general, he took a personal interest in reforming the justice system. Many French judges recommended that he abolish the jury. The judges complained that, among other problems, jurors were often illiterate or poorly educated.

Napoleon saw reasons to keep the jury, but he wanted nothing to do with a jury that was representative of the population. He agreed to maintain the jury only "if it is possible to insure its proper composition." He wanted juries to be composed of notables, social and intellectual elites, who had much to lose from chaos and disorder. He got what he wanted. His Code of Criminal Procedure of 1808 strictly limited jury service to the highly educated and well-to-do. Those eligible for jury service in each department included, for example, university graduates and the three hundred most heavily taxed citizens.

In the United States, as with eliminating property qualifications, allowing women to serve on juries was slow and uneven. Because jury service was limited to voters, women were excluded so long as they lacked the right to vote. The Nineteenth Amendment to the U.S. Constitution gave all American women the right to vote on the same basis as men in 1920, and many of the states allowed women to vote earlier. But it did not automatically follow that the right to vote led to jury service. Utah was the first state to allow women to serve on juries, in 1898. Although Wyoming gave women the right to vote in the nineteenth century, the state did not make women permanently eligible to serve on juries until 1949. By the 1940s, most states made women eligible for jury service.

Commentators gave several reasons for keeping women off juries. One was the desire to protect women from the degradation or embarrassment of hearing courtroom language or evidence. In the 1920s, a North Carolina pamphlet declared that, in courtrooms, "[p]rofanity, obscenity and the detailed narration of the lowest type of humanity are brought out in all their revolting nakedness.... Men of the South, do you like this prospect for your wife, your daughter, or for the woman who may become your wife?" This concern appeared in all regions. Besides, sequestration with male jurors might cause sexual tension. And jury service could interfere with women's responsibilities for children and the home. In 1961, women could serve on juries in forty-seven states,

5. The first all-woman jury in California was impaneled in Los Angeles in 1911. This jury acquitted the editor of the *Watts News* of printing indecent language. To form the jury pool for the case, a deputy constable summoned thirty-six women and no men.

but in nineteen of the forty-seven, a woman could claim an exemption from jury service based solely on her sex. That year, the U.S. Supreme Court upheld Florida's rule allowing women to serve on juries only if they volunteered. The Court observed that "woman is still regarded as the center of home and family life." The Court struck down such laws in 1975.

In most places, simply meeting the property requirement and other formal qualifications was not enough. Local officials often exercised considerable discretion over whom to put on jury lists. This was true of English sheriffs, and also the myriad local officials responsible for jury lists in America. Through the 1960s, many states and federal courts used the "key-man system" for compiling jury lists. In this system, jury commissioners or other local officials responsible for jury lists asked prominent members of the community—such as heads of service organizations, the chamber of commerce, and other groups—to supply names of potential jurors. The names supplied were mostly persons whom the key man knew. The argument in favor of this system was that it provided high-quality jurors. According to a 1967 survey, 60 percent of the federal district courts primarily used the key-man system, soliciting the names of "men of recognized intelligence and probity" from notables. The jurors tended to be similar to the key men: white, fairly well-to-do, and relatively well-educated.

By the 1940s, the heavily middle-class composition of most American jury lists was starting to look suspect. Millions of working-class men had been drafted and shipped off to war overseas. It seemed right that they be allowed to participate on juries. During the 1940s, the U.S. Supreme Court began to articulate what became known as the "fair cross-section requirement." In the view of the Court, representation of the full community in the jury pool was necessary to prevent discrimination "against persons of low economic and social status."

In 1968, Congress abolished the key-man system for the federal courts with the Jury Selection and Service Act. Jury lists were to be pulled randomly from voter registration lists or lists of actual voters, and supplemented if necessary through other sources of names such as driver's licenses. Following the federal act, many states also abandoned the key-man system. The number of working-class citizens, racial minorities, and women on juries rose dramatically.

The increasing computerization of jury lists, and the use of outside contractors to maintain the lists with limited supervision, can lead to problems. For example, in the 1980s, the federal jury office in Connecticut contracted with a private individual, the associate director of the Yale Computer Center, to build and maintain its jury lists. In 1989, an error caused the program for jury lists to read the "d" in Connecticut's capital city of Hartford to mean "deceased." As a result, for almost three years, no one from

Hartford received a summons for federal jury duty. The program also failed to send summonses to anyone living in New Britain, the eighth largest city in Connecticut, because the source list of names for New Britain was misplaced and never entered into the program. These two mistakes together eliminated 63 percent of voting-age Black persons and 68 percent of Hispanics in the jury district.

Other countries that use lay jurors typically draw their lists from electoral rolls. England, in particular, emphasizes that jurors are selected from the electoral register at random. England also centralizes administration of the jury system, with a Jury Central Summoning Bureau in London that summons jurors for trials throughout the country.

Before reforms, local officials not only had discretion about whom to include on jury lists, they often had discretion about whom to summon for a particular case. Both in England and the United States, this discretion led to jury packing, to get desired results in cases. In the South after Reconstruction, for many years the discretion of local officials kept Black people off juries. This was despite agitation for Black jury service in the North. Frederick Douglass, an escaped slave who became an influential campaigner for Black rights, believed that service on juries was essential for Black persons to become full citizens. In his 1892 autobiography, Douglass declared "that the liberties of the American people were dependent upon the ballot-box, the jury-box, and the cartridge-box; that without these no class of people could live and flourish in this country."

There were many ways of keeping Black people off juries. Formal disqualification was not necessary, and such provisions were rare. In 1879, the U.S. Supreme Court, interpreting the Equal Protection Clause of the Fourteenth Amendment, struck down West Virginia's statute specifying that only whites could serve as jurors. But that decision made no difference in the South to the

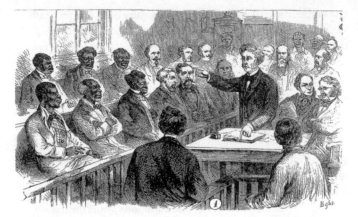

6. A racially integrated jury hears a case in the South in 1867. During Reconstruction, federal troops ensured that Black persons could serve on juries, but thereafter in the South Black jurors were rare until the 1960s.

number of Black persons serving on juries. In 1876, the *Colored Tribune* of Savannah, Georgia, suggested why: "There is not a single instance on record where a colored juror has served upon any jury in this city or County. We have been told that for eight years past, the names of colored men have been in the jury box, and these boxes have been exhausted time and again, and not one colored man's name has ever been drawn...."

In the twentieth century, Southern jury commissioners regularly put on jury lists a few Black ministers and funeral directors but left off all others. Then the sheriff or other local official had discretion about whom to summon. In 1953, in *Avery v. Georgia*, the U.S. Supreme Court struck down a Georgia practice of color-coding by race the tickets put into a box for jury selection. In a rape case, the practice led to "not a single Negro selected to serve on a panel of sixty—though many were available." Into the 1950s, African Americans sometimes served as jurors in large cities in the South, but virtually never in southern rural areas.

Who answers the summons, and excuses

Despite praise for the jury as a democratic institution, getting people to show up for jury duty has been a perennial problem. This was especially true beginning in the nineteenth century as the market economy took hold, and time became more valuable.

Jurors often have other things to do, and juror pay is low. In the United States in the nineteenth century, one sheriff was so desperate to get jurors that he rounded some up and tied them to a tree to prevent escape. In the past, many persons preferred to pay fines or bribes rather than show up when summoned. This got to be such a problem with merchants in New York City after the Civil War that the *New York Times* implored merchants to do their civic duty, or else juries would be bereft of the most knowledgeable, intelligent members of the community. In 2007, a study revealed that white residents of New York City were considerably more likely to answer a jury summons than Black, Hispanic, or Asian residents. According to the study, whites made up 78 percent of Manhattan jury pools, but were only 54 percent of the population. The different rates of response pose a challenge for the fair cross-section requirement and the idea of the jury as representative of the community.

In the United States today, judges vary widely in their willingness to accept excuses. Some jurors have been known to sneak out during jury selection and buy non-refundable plane tickets to avoid jury service. Increasingly, potential jurors make excuses before they appear in court, through advance questionnaires. A common joke is that the only people who will show up for jury duty and serve are retired people and postal service employees.

Japan, like the United States and other countries, has a serious no-show problem. In Japan, nearly 80 percent of people summoned for lay judge duty either are excused or simply do not show up on the designated day. This percentage has increased from about 60 percent at the beginning of the lay judge system in 2009. Excuses are granted liberally for difficulties such as old age, illness, work, school, and family responsibilities. As in other countries, the stipend for serving as a lay juror is low, and employers are reluctant to pay employees for missing days of work. In addition, child care at reasonable expense is hard to find. The judiciary excuses almost anyone who asks, and those who simply do not show up are never fined. In effect, the Japanese lay juror system operates on a volunteer basis. In Germany, to avoid problems getting jurors to show up, some states rely on volunteers for jury duty.

The United Kingdom takes a hard line, threatening jurors with a £1,000 fine for not showing up. The government has announced that participation by randomly chosen qualified citizens is a goal of its jury system, and its actions indicate that it is serious. In fact, the United Kingdom seems far more serious about representation of the population on the jury than the United States. It is clear that to achieve that purpose, coercion is necessary.

Questioning and challenging jurors

Even if a potential juror meets the formal qualifications for service, makes it onto the jury list, is summoned for a case, and actually shows up when summoned, some countries have a final hurdle to serving on a jury. Concern about juror partiality is longstanding. The remedy that the common law hit upon was adversarial: let the parties challenge the jurors. Each party has unlimited challenges "for cause," a specific reason. And the parties may also have a certain number of "peremptory" challenges, which can be used for any reason. A major issue concerns the scope of questioning jurors to decide whether to exercise these challenges.

English judges have curtailed the process of challenging jurors. In modern English practice, there is little questioning of potential jurors. Potential jurors are often told the names of the witnesses, and they are supposed to declare whether they know any of them, the parties, or the lawyers. Generally, a party challenging a juror for bias must present evidence of bias before any questioning can occur. Judges have wide discretion about whether to allow questioning of potential jurors and to what extent. Jury selection in England is normally swift, taking less than half a trial day, often ten minutes. Likewise, other legal systems that use lay jurors allow very little or no questioning of potential jurors. French jurors are not questioned. German jurors can be removed only for the same reasons a judge would be recused—for example, a financial interest in the case.

The process is quite different in many courts in the United States. Lawyers in England and elsewhere are amazed at the length and intrusiveness of questioning potential jurors in American courts, which can cover religious beliefs, political affiliation, charitable contributions, reading and viewing habits, medical history, and much else.

How did the United States diverge so dramatically from the process of jury selection in other countries? The key American opinion was that of Chief Justice John Marshall, acting as the presiding judge in the trial of Aaron Burr for treason in 1807. In one opinion, Marshall swept away the powerful barriers that English judges had erected to cabin the questioning of jurors. Marshall feared that the U.S. marshal, the federal official in charge of summoning the jurors, had packed Burr's jury with Jeffersonian Republicans. President Jefferson was eager to get a conviction against Burr, his former vice president, whom he hated. Federal marshals were suspected of jury packing in other political cases in the early republic. So Chief Justice Marshall permitted Burr's counsel to ask jurors questions about bias, without first showing independent evidence of bias.

A novel practice in an extraordinary political case soon spread to ordinary cases, thanks to the aggressive American bar. Voir dire, from an Anglo-Norman phrase meaning "to speak the truth," is the term for questioning potential jurors. After Burr's trial, American lawyers pushed for and won more extensive voir dire in both criminal and civil cases. In many places, lawyers used these new procedures to try to shape juries to their liking. In the process, they lengthened trial and helped to make it unworkable as a routine matter.

American lawyers especially took advantage of questioning to exercise peremptory challenges. As peremptory challenges could be used for any reason, they afforded a wide scope for questioning; the only limit was a lawyer's imagination and the judge's patience. In contrast, the English legal system remained so consistently hostile to voir dire—and to lawyers' efforts to shape juries—that peremptory challenges ultimately withered. In 1988, England abolished peremptory challenges. But the United States had a more powerful legal profession. Peremptory challenges flourished and remain today, providing an excuse for ever-expanding voir dire.

Mark Twain had views about the effects of American lawyers and voir dire on the jury. In his 1872 travel memoir, *Roughing It*, Twain described voir dire in a murder case in the Nevada Territory, in which anyone who said he had discussed or read in the newspaper about the notorious killing was struck off the jury. "Why could not the jury law be altered so as to give men of brains and honesty an equal chance with fools and miscreants? . . . I wish to so alter it as to put a premium on intelligence and character, and close the jury box against idiots, blacklegs, and people who do not read newspapers." In 1873, he declared in a Fourth of July speech in London: "We have a criminal jury system which is superior to any in the world and its efficiency is only marred by the difficulty of finding twelve men every day who don't know anything and can't read."

In the mid-twentieth century, changes to the jury pool made trial lawyers push even harder for extensive questioning of potential jurors. The fair cross-section requirement and the abolition of the key-man system made jury pools more diverse, therefore more unpredictable. In response, trial lawyers turned increasingly to specialists in jury selection: jury consultants, now called trial consultants. In the United States, trial consulting has become an industry, with its own trade association, the American Society of Trial Consultants. Trial consultants organize mock juries, elaborately analyze the jury pools that clients face, and carefully craft arguments that are likely to resonate with possible jurors. Trial consulting has become a subject of popular interest, with a TV series called *Bull* launched in 2016.

Guided by trial consultants, lawyers try to shape a jury to favor their client. Lawyers for plaintiffs in patent infringement cases tend to strike any juror who appears to be intelligent or educated. Lawyers representing individuals against corporations tend to strike jurors who are well-to-do. These examples could be multiplied almost endlessly.

Lawyer-conducted voir dire can stray far from the issues in the case. Here is an exchange between a lawyer and a potential juror in the 1997–8 trial of Terry Nichols for bombing the Oklahoma City federal building in 1995.

> Question: Are you familiar with the fact that the Cirque du Soleil is in town?
> Answer: Yes, I am.
> Question: I read from your questionnaire that you have an interest that pertains to that recreational activity.
> Answer: Yes, I do.
> Question: Would you tell us a little bit about that?
> Answer: I have a hobby of swinging on a trapeze with maybe another two dozen people with similar interests.

Jury selection in the Nichols case took over four weeks, and more than two months in O. J. Simpson's 1994–5 trial for murdering his ex-wife and her friend. Extensive voir dire is an important factor causing jury trials to grow ever longer. The lengthening of jury trial has increased pressure on civil parties to settle, and on criminal defendants to plead guilty, to spare the costs of trial. In an alleged effort to root out juror bias, the lawyers diminished jury trial.

Lengthy probing of potential jurors not only hinders efficiency, it also interferes with the idea of the jury as representative of the people. Voir dire combined with peremptory challenges, especially, allow lawyers to shape a jury to be notably different from the demographic and viewpoint range of the population. For this reason, many academics and some judges have recommended abolishing peremptory challenges. The Supreme Court of Arizona did so in 2021.

In criminal cases, it is well known that in many areas prosecutors try to strike Black Americans from the jury, and defense counsel try to strike whites. Their success in shaping the final jury depends on the composition of the jury pool. The U.S. Supreme Court has tried to stop such tactics, with limited results. In 1986, in *Batson v. Kentucky*, the Court held that striking a juror solely because of the person's race violates the Equal Protection Clause of the Fourteenth Amendment. In 1994, the Court extended the rule to strikes based on sex. (The rules apply in both civil and criminal cases.) The problem is that lawyers try to justify striking a juror by giving a race- or sex-neutral reason, and judges often accept the proffered explanation. Peremptory challenges allow lawyers to give a wide variety of reasons. In case a judge is skeptical, lawyers develop elaborate numerical strategies to disguise strikes based on race and sex.

Some Argentine provinces have addressed the question of representation of race and sex with quotas. In Argentina, the provinces may decide for themselves whether and how to use lay participation, and several have adopted the independent, all-lay jury of twelve. In all provinces that use lay participation, the final panel must consist of equal numbers of men and women, so typically six of each. And several Argentine provinces have established special juries for the trial of indigenous defendants. On such a jury, half the jurors—six people—must be members of the defendant's tribe. This type of jury resembles the historic English "jury of the half-tongue," used for the trial of foreigners; half the jury, or six members, had to be foreigners (though not necessarily from the same place as the defendant). England abolished this type of jury in 1870. Quotas of types of jurors tend to imply sharp divisions in society.

Many American trial lawyers say that a jury verdict is decided on voir dire, before any evidence is heard. That jury selection is such a critical component of adjudication by jury trial is cause for concern. It suggests that juror predispositions, or biases, are the deciding factor in a case. It is not enough to say that the two sides will cancel each other out. One side may be far better at jury selection than the other.

Providing expertise: special juries

A type of jury that used to be frequent in the common-law world is the special jury. These juries provided expertise on difficult or technical matters, and they drew from more limited pools than ordinary juries. These types of jury have gone into decline. More democratic, egalitarian ideals have discouraged special juries. But today, when evidence is increasingly complicated and in mathematical or scientific form, the idea of a special jury may be more important than ever. Even judges have difficulty with highly technical questions, and special juries could help.

Special, technical juries have a long pedigree at common law. One of the earliest was the jury of matrons, a jury composed entirely of married women whose job was to determine if a female convict was pregnant. If she was, execution would be postponed at least until the birth of the child, but often in practice indefinitely. Some of these jurors were midwives. In the mid-eighteenth century, as England was becoming a global commercial power, questions of commercial law and marine insurance became vital. These cases often turned on technical knowledge. Lord Mansfield, Chief Justice of the King's Bench, made extensive use of special juries to get these questions right. He understood the importance of accuracy of legal decisions for England's economic development. He called together juries of sea captains to decide factual questions involving marine insurance, and juries of merchants to advise on business practices. Other English judges followed his example.

In the United States, courts sometimes used special juries of educated people, often called "blue-ribbon juries," to decide complicated cases. Many states used such a procedure, but have abandoned it, some as late as the 1980s. Delaware is the only state that has retained the special jury, for use in complex civil litigation. Like Lord Mansfield's England, Delaware has a strong interest in maintaining its courts as a forum for accurate decision of commercial cases.

Today, some of the most complicated cases involve intellectual property, especially patent infringement. The technologies can be so complicated that judges have trouble understanding them, much less ordinary jurors. Some persons have proposed using special, technically trained juries in patent cases. Such proposals highlight the tension between ordinary juries and the desire for modern expertise. This is an example of the many tensions involved in jury selection, which careful attention to the purposes of the jury can help to resolve.

Chapter 5
The scope and form of the jury

A visitor to France walks into a courtroom and sees, at the far end, a wide, high judicial bench with twelve people sitting there. A person in the middle is wearing a scarlet robe with white fur trim; on either side of him is a man and a woman in black robes. The other nine people on the bench are in ordinary clothes, four on one side of the robed trio and five on the other. The visitor wonders what kind of court this is. It is a mixed court of three professional judges and nine lay jurors. Juror participation can look quite different around the globe, and jurors can be used to make different kinds of decisions.

The U.S. Supreme Court has laid down some rigid rules, binding on the entire country, about when juries must be used and how. Other common-law countries—such as England and many of its former colonies—are more flexible, and civil-law countries have proved the most innovative of all. Civil-law systems have developed the mixed panel of professional judges and lay jurors. Not bound by tradition or by inflexible constitutional rules, some civil-law systems have succeeded in introducing lay participation into a greater share of cases than the United States has. The strict rules in the United States have, to a large extent, backfired and encouraged plea bargaining. Fewer cases are going to juries, or any adjudication at all.

Around the world, the use of lay jurors is typically reserved for criminal cases, and only the most serious of those. Using lay jurors has considerable costs, including summoning the jurors, instructing them on the law and the evidence, and taking the jurors away from their normal activities. Given these costs, most legal systems reserve the use of jurors for cases in which they are thought to be most needed. For example, the French legal system uses lay jurors for deciding cases of murder, rape, armed robbery, kidnapping, counterfeiting, torture, and terrorism. In Japan, lay jurors decide mainly homicide cases and a few others, totaling 1.5 percent of all crimes charged. Likewise, common-law countries such as England and Wales, Australia, Canada, Jamaica, and New Zealand have saved the use of juries for serious criminal cases. Those countries have all virtually abolished the civil jury.

The United States is the outlier. At least in theory, it requires jury trial both for many civil cases and for many minor criminal offenses. In criminal cases, the U.S. Supreme Court has applied the Sixth Amendment of the Constitution to the states. The relevant part of the Sixth Amendment states: "In all criminal prosecutions, the accused shall enjoy the right to a speedy and public trial, by an impartial jury...." In applying this provision to the states, the Court laid down a rule about when criminal jury trial is required: for all offenses for which the maximum punishment is more than six months' imprisonment. This group includes many misdemeanors, such as the simple battery (touching or hitting someone) at issue in the case that established the rule, *Duncan v. Louisiana* (1968).

Applying such a strict rule to the whole country seemed like a good idea at the time. The case involved racial tensions, and evoked concerns about the poor treatment of Black defendants in the South. Duncan was a 19-year-old Black man accused of slapping a white boy. Under Louisiana law at the time, the case was a misdemeanor and thus not subject to trial by jury. A judge convicted Duncan and sentenced him to sixty days' imprisonment and a fine of $150. The Supreme Court was likely concerned that a judge might be racially biased and so required jury trial.

But, as well-intentioned as it was, the rule of *Duncan v. Louisiana* is subject to the law of unintended consequences. A holding that was intended to correct racial bias among the judiciary by giving misdemeanor defendants a right to jury trial has resulted in almost no trials whatsoever. Jury trials have become so expensive and unpredictable that they are unworkable for routine cases. Prosecutors vastly prefer to offer plea bargains, especially in misdemeanor cases, and defendants take them because of the discount in punishment. A plea bargain is a deal in which a prosecutor offers a lesser charge or a lesser sentence in exchange for the defendant confessing guilt, or "pleading guilty." This deal saves the trouble of a jury trial. Legislatures have encouraged plea bargaining by changing sentencing policies. The United States today holds very few trials relative to the number of criminal convictions. At least a conviction by a judge could be appealed, as Duncan did. But there is almost no appeal from a plea bargain.

Size of the jury

Since the thirteenth century, twelve has been the traditional number of jurors in the common-law world. Why twelve? The number twelve is biblical. There were twelve tribes of Israel, and Christ chose twelve apostles, whom Christ said would sit on twelve thrones to judge the twelve tribes. Twelve therefore represents the perfect government of God. This symbolism helped to smooth the transition from the judgment of God, in the ordeals, to the judgment of men. The jurors represented divine authority. And, as the nineteenth-century English judge and criminologist Sir James Fitzjames Stephen pointed out, twelve is a number that forms "a group just large enough to destroy even the appearance of individual responsibility."

Later, as the market economy grew and time became more valuable, many Americans did not want to spend precious time deciding other people's cases. This was especially true of civil cases. As a delegate to the New York Constitutional Convention of 1846 put it: "I would respect the just rights of all litigants, but at the same time remember that men who are not litigants have rights also and ought not to be dragged from their own business by the dozens to settle other people's quarrels...." Delegates to state constitutional conventions also complained about the costs to counties of summoning enough potential jurors to impanel twelve for each case and of paying the jurors for their service.

For these reasons, beginning in the mid-nineteenth century many states began to allow fewer than twelve jurors in civil cases. In criminal cases, too, states began to use juries of fewer than twelve. The states that allowed such smaller juries typically did so in misdemeanor cases, but a few also permitted it for more serious cases. This trend grew in the 1960s, and the timing was not an accident. Because of soaring rates of violent crime, especially robbery and homicide in cities, state courts were struggling to cope with a flood of new criminal cases. One possible solution was to use smaller juries. Fewer jurors meant cost savings, less deliberation time, and fewer hung juries. Some states eagerly grasped at this lifeline—anything to process cases faster.

But there was a potential glitch: the U.S. Supreme Court. In the 1968 *Duncan* case, the Supreme Court applied the Sixth Amendment right to criminal jury trial to the states. This raised a tricky question. Did the Sixth Amendment require the states to use twelve jurors? After all, that was the federal practice.

The Court answered that question in 1970, in the case of *Williams v. Florida*. Florida used a jury of six for all criminal cases except capital ones. Williams was tried for robbery by a jury of six, convicted, and sentenced to life imprisonment. The U.S. Supreme Court upheld his conviction. In reaching this result, the Court declared that the purpose of criminal jury trial was to prevent oppression by the government. This, the Court announced, could be done as well by a six-person as by a twelve-person jury. The number twelve, the Court stated, was a "historical accident" and explanations for it rested "on little more than mystical or superstitious insights." The Court cited empirical studies on the effects of different numbers of jurors and found "no discernable difference" in the results.

In its eagerness to allow states to find ways to cope with the new torrent of criminal cases, the Court misinterpreted the studies. For example, the Court stated that the ratio of the majority to dissent on a jury was the key to strength of the dissent, rather than the absolute number of dissenters. The Court therefore supposed that in a jury divided 5–1, the dissenter would be equally able to withstand the majority as the dissenters in a jury divided 10–2. In fact, the empirical studies that the Court cited showed the opposite. Having more than one juror in dissent made a difference. Since then, much empirical work has been done on the effects of jury size. Besides the finding that twelve-person civil juries tend to be more moderate and predictable in awarding damages, larger juries have other consistent features. On a larger jury, there is a greater chance that someone will recall relevant evidence. Larger juries are less likely to be dominated by a single assertive juror. And larger juries are more likely to contain a representative cross-section of the community. A jury of six is both less likely to contain a member of a significant minority group and more likely to have unrepresentatively large numbers of minorities. When a jury lacks members of different groups, there is often less consideration of different views, and it is less likely that jurors will overcome various types of bias.

The rule of *Williams* still stands. The U.S. Supreme Court did, at least, put a floor on the number of jurors required by the Sixth Amendment. Five was too few, the Court declared in the 1978 case *Ballew v. Georgia*, and almost seemed to be making amends for its prior misinterpretation of empirical studies by discussing research showing the advantages of larger juries.

In criminal cases, federal courts continue to require juries of twelve. Many other common-law countries—England, Canada, Australia, and New Zealand—have retained a jury of twelve in criminal cases. Jamaica uses a jury of twelve for murder or treason cases, but a jury of seven for other criminal cases. Among civil-law countries with independent lay juries (not a mixed panel), several Argentine provinces use a jury of twelve, Spain uses a jury of nine, Russia uses eight, Brazil seven, and South Korea uses five, seven, or nine jurors depending on the seriousness of the crime.

Unanimity

Larger juries have advantages, but they sometimes make it more difficult to achieve unanimity. Traditionally, the common-law jury had to be unanimous. The phrase "By God and by my country" that an English criminal defendant used to accept jury trial is significant. To ease the difficulty of moving from the judgment of God to the judgment of men, the decision of the jury was equated with both divine judgment and the mystical voice of the country. Because of this representation, all members of the jury had to agree on the decision. The judgment of God could not be divided, nor could the mystical voice of the country.

The problem was that there might well be different opinions on the jury. The jurors would need encouragement to reach unanimity. The English common-law system supplied that encouragement. As the seventeenth-century judge and legal writer Sir Edward Coke described, during deliberations, jurors were kept in the custody of a marshal or bailiff "without meat [food] or drinke, fire or candle" and without speaking to anyone else until they reached a unanimous verdict. Until they all agreed, they were uncomfortable prisoners—sometimes hungry, thirsty, freezing, and

7. Thomas Rownlandson's 1815 print *A Lamentable Case of a Jury-Man* ridicules the strict confinement of jurors. A juror has soiled himself.

Judge: "Mr. Juryman, you have requested permission to retire for a few moments. I have been looking some time for a precedent, and have at last found, by the 25 of William Rufus [reigned 1087–1100], Chap. 53, that a Juryman, on any urgent occasion, may retire backwards for the space of ten minutes only. Therefore you may withdraw."

Juror: "I am much obliged to your Lordship for the trouble you have taken—but it has been all over these five minutes!"

Fellow jurors: "Brother, we are perfectly convinced of the truth of your assertion!!"

in the dark. The jury system rested on multiple levels of coercion, forcing jurors first to appear, then to deliberate to unanimity.

Jurors were kept as prisoners even before deliberations, in fact as soon as they were sworn. Not surprisingly, they sometimes tried to escape. In a 1499 civil case, jurors hearing evidence took advantage of a tremendous thunderstorm to run out of the hall where the trial was being held, without permission of the judges, supposedly because they were frightened. Despite his terror, one of the jurors kept his wits enough to take shelter from the downpour in an alehouse. There he was given a free drink and told that the defendants had the better case. After the excitement was over, the jury eventually came back, heard the rest of the evidence, and gave a verdict for the plaintiffs. Even though the verdict was for the plaintiffs, the juror's drink in the alehouse was considered so serious that the matter was heard by all the twelve judges of England, to determine the proper consequences. Jurors were routinely fined, and sometimes imprisoned, for eating or drinking before giving their verdict.

The discomfort of the jurors during the proceedings helps to explain the astonishing speed of common-law trials and deliberations. In the eighteenth century, an English judge often presided over more than a dozen felony trials, with verdicts, per day. Parties would not want to try the patience of hungry, thirsty jurors with overlong presentations. And jurors had incentive to agree on a verdict as quickly as possible. Following a civil verdict, it was customary—and lawful—for the winning party to provide the jurors a good dinner. And criminal juries, their duties discharged with a verdict, were free to eat afterwards. Alexander Pope, in his 1714 poem *The Rape of the Lock*, wrote that "wretches hang that jurymen may dine." The rule against food and drink helped to make common-law adversarial jury trial fast enough to be workable as a routine matter. Later ages did not apply this kind of pressure, and adversarial jury trial became hopelessly slow. During the nineteenth century, the rule was relaxed and effectively ended. Trials lengthened, and the problem of hung juries arose.

Another way that the common law encouraged unanimity was through the strong figure of the jury foreman, later foreperson. In the mid-fifteenth century, concern about bribery of jurors had heightened, and the Crown was eager to have a man of substance and authority on the jury. The jury foreman emerged and gradually evolved into a sort of office. By the mid-seventeenth century, certain men served as repeat foremen and took a special oath that was different from that of other jurors. In one example, in Kent in the mid-seventeenth century, over the course of thirteen years Robert Day served as a juror in at least 118 trials, 111 of them as foreman. Their high standing in the community and repeat service meant that foremen were deeply familiar with the legal system and influential with their fellow jurors. They could help guide the jury to a swift verdict.

Americans imported this role, and today the foreperson is usually responsible for organizing discussion during deliberations, announcing breaks, and keeping track of votes. In the United States, the foreperson is generally selected by one of three methods: appointment by the judge; election by fellow jurors; or random selection. Of these methods, the most common is appointment by the judge. While selection as the foreperson does tend to confer greater influence with the jury, that authority is considerably weaker than the clout of the earlier repeat foremen.

With the end of the virtual imprisonment of jurors and the decline of the foreperson's authority, jury unanimity is harder to achieve. Deliberations take longer and hung juries have become more common. A study has shown that, during the 1980s and 1990s, rates of hung juries in criminal cases averaged 2.5 percent in federal court and in felony cases in state court averaged 6.2 percent, with much wider variation: 0.1 percent in Pierce County, Washington, to 14.8 percent in Los Angeles County, California. Juries in Washington, DC, have hung at a rate of 22 percent. Retrial is expensive; the costs of a hung jury are high.

In 2020, in *Ramos v. Louisiana*, the U.S. Supreme Court held that the Sixth Amendment required that criminal jury verdicts be unanimous. The Court's decision discussed the common-law tradition of unanimity, and concerns that, with a non-unanimous verdict, the views of racial minorities on the jury would be sidelined. At the time of the Court's decision, only two states allowed non-unanimous verdicts in criminal cases.

In the rest of the common-law world, most countries have adopted non-unanimous verdicts. Canada continues to require unanimity in criminal cases. But other countries have changed. In 1967, legislation in England allowed criminal juries to return a verdict of 10–2. The jury has to deliberate at least two hours before the judge will accept a non-unanimous verdict. In 1981, New Zealand permitted an 11–1 verdict in a criminal case, but only after the jury has deliberated at least four hours. In Australia, all states now permit non-unanimous verdicts, with most allowing verdicts of 10–2. Three Australian states still require a unanimous verdict in murder cases. Jamaica permits a verdict of 9–3 for certain categories of murder, after the jury has deliberated at least two hours.

Because of different voting rules, civil-law countries that use lay jurors do not face the problem of a hung jury. Like most common-law countries, civil-law countries do not require unanimity. But unlike common-law countries, after deliberations, the panel takes one formal vote, sometimes by secret ballot. If the threshold number of votes for a conviction is not reached, the defendant is acquitted. In those systems, the prosecution as well as the defense can appeal, so the problem of a false acquittal is not so great.

The main arguments against unanimity are the problems of longer deliberations and hung juries, with the subsequent cost of retrial to the parties and victims. These are the reasons why so many other common-law countries, and virtually all civil-law countries, allow for non-unanimous verdicts. The proponents of unanimity argue that unanimous verdicts lead to greater public confidence in the accuracy of the verdict and reinforce the standard of proof for conviction of beyond a reasonable doubt. Further, allowing non-unanimous verdicts tends to make jury deliberations less thorough, and sometimes encourages disregard of minority views.

In the United States, it is a serious question whether the requirement of criminal jury unanimity, combined with a diverse jury pool in many places, has increased the threat of a hung jury and therefore encouraged more plea bargains to avoid jury trial. The result of requiring jury unanimity might be, in some cases, no jury trial at all.

Juries in civil-law countries: the mixed panel

One of the most important innovations in the use of lay jurors has come from the civil-law systems: the mixed panel, composed of both professional judges and lay jurors, who hear evidence together, deliberate together, and vote together on guilt and sentence. The mixed panel has come to be the dominant form of lay participation in civil-law countries, as it prevents many perceived problems with the common-law independent jury.

How did this novel arrangement come about? The original French jury, which started during the Revolution, was a jury composed of lay persons only. Many other governments followed the French model when they first adopted juries, including the German states. But one of these, Hanover, adopted a different model. In 1850, Hanoverian legislation provided for criminal courts of one professional judge and two lay jurors (technically "lay judges") sitting together. This system soon spread throughout the German states. At first, these mixed panels were used only for petty crimes.

But in 1931, both Germany and Italy adopted a mixed panel of professional judges and lay jurors for serious criminal cases. Both systems proved surprisingly durable and continue today. In Germany, a mixed panel of one professional judge and two lay jurors (the *Schöffengericht*) decides lesser crimes; and a mixed panel of three professional judges and two lay jurors (the *grosse Strafkammer*) decides more serious crimes. A vote to convict requires a two-thirds majority, so four votes for the more serious crimes.

In 1941, the Vichy regime in France introduced the mixed tribunal, which France has maintained to this day. This change did not come out of the blue, or solely in response to German pressure. It could hardly have lasted so long if it had. Throughout the nineteenth century and into the twentieth, complaints persisted that all-lay juries were too lenient toward criminal defendants, confused by evidence, and apt to nullify the law. The mixed panel seemed an excellent way to preserve the rule of law and to ensure better competence concerning facts, while retaining lay participation.

In the French court using the mixed panel, the *Cour d'assises*, nine lay jurors sit on the bench with three professional judges to hear evidence, and the panel deliberates and votes together. Votes are taken by secret ballot, and eight votes are needed to convict.

By the early 1980s, all over Europe the all-lay jury was abandoned or sharply limited—replaced by either professional judges or the mixed panel. The jury had been the banner of the nineteenth-century liberal movement, with its insistence that tribunals represent the people. But during the twentieth century, priorities changed. Predictability and expertise became more important. A few European countries have revived all-lay juries in the 1990s—notably Spain and Russia. But the all-lay jury is deeply incompatible with civil-law systems, which aspire to adherence to law and careful evaluation of fact, with reasons for decisions explained and provision for a thorough appeal.

Ironically, many of the systems using mixed panels have managed to preserve lay participation in a greater percentage of criminal cases than the United States. And these lay jurors have influence over sentences as well as determinations of guilt.

The role of lay jurors in sentencing is a major area of difference between common-law and civil-law countries. In common-law countries, the jury is almost always limited to deciding the question of guilt. Sentencing is left to the judge alone. The narrow exceptions are capital punishment and, in a very few American states, other sentences. In many American courts today, judges are forbidden to tell jurors about the sentences for different crimes. This restriction helps to prevent the jurors from nullifying the law. But it also leaves jurors in the dark about the consequences of their verdict for the sentence.

In civil-law countries, by contrast, lay jurors decide the sentence as well as guilt. Those two decisions are not separated, as in common-law countries. The mixed panels decide both questions together, during the same session of deliberations. Some commentators are concerned that the professional judges on mixed panels have so much influence over lay jurors that the lay jurors are superfluous. But studies have shown that lay jurors do have an effect on sentencing. One study of German courts, for example, indicated that sometimes professional judges compromised with lay jurors concerning the punishment. At times the lay jurors were harsher than the professional judge or judges, but somewhat more often they were more lenient toward the defendant. In various cases in the study, the lay jurors sympathized with the defendant because the defendant was young, had a hard childhood, was in financial difficulties, was epileptic, or was drunk at the time of the offense. In general, the lay jurors were apt to be harsher than the professional judges toward sex offenders, a result also seen in Japan.

Some civil-law countries have found ways to incorporate lay jurors more thoroughly into their criminal justice systems than the United States, with its long historical tradition of the jury and its constitutional rights to jury trial. Flexibility and innovation have proved to be the keys to lay participation.

Chapter 6
Limitations of lay jurors

In *The Federalist* No. 83, Alexander Hamilton wrote of his personal "high estimation" of the criminal jury, and declared that "all are satisfied of the utility of the institution, and of its friendly aspect to liberty." But, as Hamilton knew, legal systems that use juries have had to manage, one way or another, the inevitable limitations and drawbacks. As Tocqueville pointed out, it is not easy to adapt an institution that originated in a much simpler society to complex societies today. Juries sometimes have difficulty understanding judicial instructions and complicated evidence, are susceptible to emotional appeals, may be biased, deliberate in secret without accountability, and require concentrated trial of all issues at once. Jurors endure hardships, including long trials, financial costs, and disruption of work and family life.

Lay jurors, who are chosen from the people and are not legal professionals, have limited time, capacity, and knowledge for resolving disputes. That is why so many serious thinkers about the jury have stressed the importance of narrowing the jury's decision to a limited number of facts, and the application of law to facts. They have pointed out that any dispute decided by the people must be radically simplified. As Montesquieu put it, "the people are not jurists... they must be presented with a single object, a deed, and only one deed...." Alexander Hamilton agreed. He explained: "The simplicity and expedition which form the distinguishing characters of this mode of trial [by jury] require, that the matter to be decided should be reduced to some single and obvious point."

English common-law judges shared these concerns about adjudication by lay jurors. At every turn, the common law was shaped by the need to simplify cases for the jury. This drastic simplification occurred even if that meant sacrificing accuracy of decision-making, as some disputes were unavoidably complicated. Medieval English judges required lawyers for both sides to simplify their civil cases until they arrived at a single factual issue in dispute. This process was called "pleading to issue," and it took place under the guidance of the judges, at first orally and then in writing. Over time, this requirement was slightly relaxed, but still, judges allowed only a few factual issues to go to a jury at a time. Courts strictly limited the number of claims that could be heard at once and the number of parties to a dispute. Remedies at common law became increasingly limited to money damages, which were easy to announce, rather than requiring the defendant to take certain actions (called specific performance).

Because of the need to radically simplify cases for the jury, England had to develop a separate, non-jury legal system to deal with more complicated cases. Otherwise, the jury system would have produced many more grave injustices.

In the late eighteenth century, in both England and America, the cases that went to civil juries were fairly simple. Mostly they concerned ownership of land and debt collection. These cases needed few witnesses and seldom involved complicated questions of law or fact. The simplified types of cases that went to a jury, together with property requirements and homogenous New England jurors, led John Adams to comment in 1771 that "the general rules of law and common regulations of society" are "well enough known to ordinary jurors."

Despite such assurances, over time there has been considerable doubt whether many jurors understand or are able to reasonably apply legal concepts, and how far they understand evidence.

In the mid-eighteenth century, Blackstone praised the jury as "the glory of the English law" that has "secured the just liberties of this nation for a long succession of ages." But by the mid-nineteenth century, English authors and artists mocked the jury as a comical institution. In 1846, the English humorist Gilbert Abbott à Beckett wrote a popular parody of Blackstone's *Commentaries*. One chapter is a send-up of Blackstone's effusive chapter on the civil jury. Beckett declared that the arguments of opposing counsel cause "much bewilderment to the jurymen, who are further puzzled by the summing up of the judge, the usher's cries for silence, and the perpetual talking of the briefless barristers." Although it "would be right down blasphemy to doubt the integrity of a British jury, . . . we have nevertheless heard of that great bulwark of our liberties tossing up [flipping a coin] occasionally, when a verdict could not be otherwise agreed on."

In *Alice's Adventures in Wonderland* (1865), Lewis Carroll portrays the jurors in the trial of the Knave of Hearts as a group of small animals. The creatures are busily writing on slates before the trial begins, and the Gryphon explains to Alice that they are writing down their names, so that they will not forget them when the trial is over. Alice exclaims, "Stupid things!" and sees the jurors then write "Stupid things!" on their slates, though one has to ask his neighbor how to spell "stupid."

In W. S. Gilbert and Arthur Sullivan's 1875 operetta *Trial by Jury*, the jury must decide a civil case for breach of promise to marry. Before the trial begins, the usher urges the jury to pay attention to the jilted plaintiff and to ignore the "ruffianly defendant." Nevertheless the usher declares, "From bias free of every kind, this trial must be tried!" The jurors greet the defendant by shaking their fists at him and threatening: "Monster, dread our damages.

8. In Lewis Carroll's *Alice's Adventures in Wonderland* (1865), Alice accidentally knocks over the jury box at the Knave of Hearts's trial.

We're the Jury, dread our fury!" The jurors pity the plaintiff, Angelina, who arrives in a wedding dress. In her distress, and desire for damages, Angelina swoons first into the arms of the foreman of the jury and then into the arms of the judge. The case ends with "joy unbounded" when the judge offers to marry Angelina himself.

American authors and artists joined in. The antiquity of the jury had been a great mark in its favor during the American Revolution and at the founding of the republic. But by the late nineteenth century, the institution's age, far from being a benefit, was viewed as a liability. At that time, the story was current that jury trial had been founded by the ninth-century Anglo-Saxon king Alfred the Great. In 1872, Mark Twain commented on Alfred's supposed invention. "Alfred the Great, when he invented trial by jury and knew that he had admirably framed it to secure justice in his age of the world, was not aware that in the nineteenth century the condition of things would be so entirely changed that unless he rose from the grave and altered the jury plan to meet the emergency, it would prove the most ingenious and infallible agency for defeating justice that human wisdom could contrive." Twain went on: "For how could he imagine that we simpletons would go on using his jury plan after circumstances had stripped it of its usefulness, any more than he could imagine that we would go on using his candle-clock after we had invented chronometers?"

Newspapers and law reviews took up the refrain. The *New York Times* declared in 1871: "It was a rude age when Alfred flourished, and the jury trial in its first crude form was a vast improvement on the old method of testing a man's innocence by his ability to hold a hot iron unscorched, or walk barefooted over shards and flints without flinching...." But, the *Times* went on, there was no reason why the jury should be "consecrated thenceforth from any attempt to improve its efficiency." The *Times* was particularly concerned with incorrect verdicts followed by endless new trials. As an example of problems with jury trial, the *Times* reported a North Carolina case in which a drunk man had stumbled onto railroad tracks and lay there in the middle of the night, far from any buildings or lights. That night a train ran him over, killing him, and the jury awarded large damages to the man's relatives for the engineer's negligence in not stopping the train. In 1904, the *Atchison* (Kansas) *Globe* related that a visitor from India came to the United States to study its institutions and visited the courthouse. "'What's the jury for?' he inquired. 'To decide which side has the better lawyer,' his guide replied." In the 1920s and 1930s, as automobile accident cases clogged American courts, academics and some lawyers called for abolition of the civil jury.

The complexity of modern cases compounds juries' challenges in understanding and applying facts and law. The United States today has rejected the longstanding practice of formally simplifying cases for the jury. In part, complication is inevitable given changes in technology and society. Even in 1852, Justice Robert Grier of the U.S. Supreme Court wrote in a patent case, over which he presided as trial judge, "cases frequently occur, in which ten out of twelve jurors do not understand the principles of science, mathematics, or philosophy, necessary to a correct judgment of the case." Grier acknowledged that judges had difficulty with these cases as well; he recommended court-appointed experts to help judges.

If that was true in 1852, the situation is much worse today. Increasingly, evidence is presented in scientific or numerical form. Jurors are called on to understand the nuances of DNA testing or ballistics in criminal cases, cutting-edge technologies in patent cases, and complicated financial transactions in fraud or contract cases. Some cases are well beyond the understanding of ordinary jurors; indeed, they are beyond the understanding of many judges, unless they have assistance from nonpartisan specialists. Evaluating such evidence does not play to the strengths of ordinary jurors.

If jurors cannot understand the relevant evidence or scientific concepts, they tend to substitute concepts they are familiar with. A juror in O. J. Simpson's murder trial equated DNA evidence with blood-typing (O positive, A negative, etc.). The jury acquitted Simpson, who later essentially admitted his guilt in a book titled *If I Did It*. In a case of a claim of patent infringement for using computer program algorithms, the plaintiff's lawyers—with the help of trial consultants—realized that the technology left mock jurors hopelessly confused. The plaintiff also brought a claim for trade dress infringement, that is, that the defendant copied the packaging or look of another company's product in order to confuse a buyer. The mock jurors understood that claim much better. One said that she had a similar problem when she went to CVS and tried to find the shampoo she liked, but other companies copied the bottle's design and confused her. In the actual trial, the plaintiff's lawyers heavily emphasized the trade dress claim and downplayed the patent claim, which was really the key issue. The jury's understanding of the trade dress claim encouraged them to give a verdict for the plaintiff on the patent claim. Much of the work of trial consultants today concerns how to simplify a case for a jury.

Sometimes the jury is so baffled that it cannot decide the case. In a 1978 case in federal court in California, plaintiff corporations claimed that IBM monopolized certain markets in the computer industry. The case involved complicated technology and financial arrangements. Following five months of trial, the jury deliberated more than three weeks and then announced that it could not reach a verdict. Before declaring a mistrial, the judge questioned the jurors about their knowledge of the case. It emerged that the jurors were bewildered by concepts such as software, interface, and barriers to entry in a market—all key to deciding the case.

Expert testimony can be especially confusing for jurors. In the twentieth century, the effect of expert testimony on lay jurors concerned European writers. Problems with jurors evaluating expert testimony are even more intense in a highly adversarial system such as the United States. The lawyers for the parties retain their own expert witnesses and coach them heavily. (The euphemism is "prepare.") Such partisan witnesses say what the lawyers want them to say; he who pays the piper calls the tune. As a result, jurors often hear expert testimony from different witnesses that is diametrically opposed. They have no independent means of evaluating these contradictory assertions, and often rely instead on how likable and non-condescending an expert seems to be, or how closely the expert's story matches something they believe or understand.

Not only do jurors have trouble understanding complicated scientific or financial testimony, they also have difficulty understanding the law. Studies consistently show that jurors do not understand many common instructions from judges about the law. This includes instructions on the typical standard of proof in a criminal case, "beyond a reasonable doubt." Some jurors understand this to mean absolute, mathematical certainty. And some jurors create other requirements. In 2008 in Orlando, Florida, a two-year-old girl named Caylee Anthony disappeared. Her maternal grandmother reported that she was missing, that her mother's car smelled as if it had contained a dead body, and that the mother had given different explanations for the girl's whereabouts, eventually admitting that she had not seen her for weeks. The mother, Casey Anthony, was arrested and told officers that Caylee had been kidnapped by a nanny and that she had been trying to find her daughter, but was too frightened to notify the police. The girl's decomposed remains were found in a laundry bag in the woods near the house where the mother had been living. The jurors acquitted Anthony of all homicide charges, but convicted her of four misdemeanor charges of providing false information to a law enforcement officer. In post-trial interviews, jurors explained that a key reason for the jury's decision was that the prosecution did not prove the exact cause of death with certainty. That would have been difficult, given the child's skeletal remains.

Historically, jurors have had particular problems with the concept of criminal intent. In the 1790s, French judges complained that jurors often confused criminal intent, acting deliberately to commit a crime, with motivation, the reason for committing a crime. The French judges could see this confusion more clearly than others because jurors had to answer detailed questions about their findings.

Concern has arisen in various countries about jurors' lack of understanding. In 2014, the Chief Justice of Trinidad and Tobago, Ivor Archie, proposed abolishing the independent jury there. Two former chief justices agreed. Archie was concerned that juries have trouble understanding judicial instructions, and indeed worried about their "functional literacy." In Trinidad and Tobago, most educated professionals are exempt from jury service. The Chief Justice discussed a murder case in which the foreman of the jury misunderstood the word "unanimous" and incorrectly reported a guilty verdict. Rather than use independent juries, the Chief Justice preferred that the nation adopt use of trained lay assessors sitting with judges in a mixed panel.

Today, sometimes jurors' confusion is because the law is more complicated, more nuanced that it was before. But often American judges' instructions are unnecessarily bewildering. Before the mid-twentieth century, trial judges' instructions were usually in ordinary English and closely tailored to the particular case. This discretion worried appellate judges; they grew concerned about trial judges' potential bias as well as imprecision. Appellate courts have endlessly tinkered with jury instructions, producing "pattern instructions" that a trial court can give and be sure to be upheld. But appellate courts have not worried much about linguistic clarity; pattern instructions are often an editor's nightmare, filled with double negatives, confusing prepositional phrases, and highly technical definitions. A trial judge's instructions in a case can occupy a thick binder. When an American judge gives instructions, the judge typically drones on and on, spewing out a set of appellate-approved instructions that a legally trained person would have trouble understanding, much less lay jurors. Jurors can usually take a set of written instructions with them into deliberations, only to puzzle over them there. When jurors ask the trial judge for help understanding these impenetrable instructions, judges often simply repeat the instructions in the same words and tell jurors to do their best. Some states have made an effort to clarify pattern instructions, but juror confusion remains. American appellate courts have achieved almost total control over jury instructions, at the price of the jury being baffled.

But the boredom and murkiness of American judges' instructions suit most lawyers. They are free to make emotional appeals to jurors, unchecked by any clear curb.

Susceptibility to emotional appeals

The susceptibility of jurors to emotional appeals is a widespread and frequent concern. Soon after jury trials began in France in the 1790s, French judges complained about jurors' gullible weakness for the eloquence of defense lawyers. In 1874 the U.S. Supreme Court, along with other American courts, expressed concern about jurors' "ignorance of the rules of law and of evidence" and verdicts founded on "impulse of passion or prejudice." In his 1949 book, *Courts on Trial*, American judge Jerome Frank gave a withering critique of the criminal and civil jury. Among his criticisms: "Many juries in reaching their verdicts act on their emotional responses to the lawyers and witnesses; . . . they do like an artful lawyer for the plaintiff, the poor widow, the brunette with the soulful eyes, and they do dislike the big corporation, the Italian with a thick, foreign accent."

Judges may be susceptible too, being human, but they are viewed as typically better able to set emotions aside. Judges are usually experienced, at least more so than most jurors, and have seen similar cases before. Legal training encourages close attention to application of law to facts. And judges are more accountable than jurors. They have incentives to pay some attention to the facts and law. Judges are named as the decision-maker, either alone or in a small group, and generally have to give written reasons for their decisions. Judges usually care about their decisions being reversed by an appellate court, and they often are concerned about their reputation among other judges and lawyers. Jurors lack almost all of these characteristics.

Lawyers seem to think there is a difference between judge and jury. Lawyers and legal scholars have commented on the difference between lawyers' tactics and rhetoric in a jury trial as opposed to a bench trial, before a judge; lawyers in a bench trial are typically more businesslike and focused on the facts and law.

Some of the judges who have been most concerned about the effect of lawyers' emotional appeals on jurors were themselves talented advocates before juries. In an opinion in 1830, Thomas Ruffin, a prominent judge of the North Carolina Supreme Court, worried about the effects on juries of "the false glosses of powerful advocates." He knew whereof he spoke; as a successful lawyer, at times he had become so excited during trials that he knocked the floor instead of the table with his knuckles.

American artists, including Winslow Homer and Thomas Nast, expressed concern about the effects of lawyers' emotional rhetoric on juries. An illustration by Nast shows a lawyer as a fox throwing dust into the eyes of jurors, portrayed as geese. Mass publications such as *Harper's Weekly* prominently displayed this art, spreading anxiety about the legal profession and the institution of the jury.

Judges, lawyers, and other commentators have complained that criminal juries were and are too lenient, failing to convict defendants who are obviously guilty. In France in the 1790s, in ordinary, non-political criminal cases, acquittal rates ranged between 40 and 50 percent. The French government believed that juries were significantly responsible for the huge increase in crime during that time. Members of the legislature called juries "the safeguard of brigands" rather than the safeguard of liberty. French

9. Thomas Nast's illustration for the cover of *Harper's Weekly*, March 29, 1873, portrays the game of fox and geese, his view of the jury trials of the period. The fox-lawyer dominates the courtroom; he throws dust from a box marked "Dust. Alias Eloquence" in the eyes of the geese-jurors, who are blinded by it. In the upper-left corner a small dog, the judge, looks on timidly.

jurors often sympathized with the accused, an emotion that defense counsel encouraged. Similar situations were reported in Russia and Germany in the nineteenth century. Both before the Russian Revolution of 1917 and after the revival of juries in the late twentieth century, Russian juries have been particularly lenient in cases involving drunken defendants. Although voluntary intoxication was supposed to be an aggravating factor according to the law, Russian juries treated it as a mitigating factor.

In England and the United States as well, studies have found jury leniency in criminal cases. In 1966, a study showed that disagreements between judges and juries were concentrated in cases in which the judge thought that there should be a conviction, but the jury acquitted.

In India, concern about the competence and bias of jurors in criminal cases caused the jury's demise. In 1931, Mohandas Karamchand (Mahatma) Gandhi warned about the difficulties of jury trial, and urged a future independent India to avoid it. An English-trained barrister, he wrote:

> I am unconvinced of the advantages of jury trials over those by judges.... When passions are roused, juries are affected by them and give perverse verdicts.... In matters where absolute impartiality, calmness and ability to sift evidence and understand human nature are required, we may not replace trained judges by untrained men brought together by chance. What we must aim at is an incorruptible, impartial and able judiciary right from the bottom.

Despite Gandhi's warning, after India became independent from the United Kingdom in 1947, various Indian states maintained the institution of the jury. But the Nanavati trial in 1959 caused many Indians to question whether jury trial should continue. The case riveted the attention of the entire country, much as the O. J. Simpson trial did in the United States in 1994–5.

Kawas Nanavati was a commander in the Indian Navy and a Parsi, a member of a group of Zoroastrians who had left Iran following the Muslim conquest there and had long been settled in India. Parsis tend to be well-educated professionals—doctors, lawyers, and so on. While he was on naval training in Portsmouth,

Nanavati married an Englishwoman, Sylvia King. The couple lived in Bombay (now Mumbai) and had three children.

In 1959, shortly after Nanavati got home from a two-month naval cruise, Sylvia told him that she had been having an affair with Prem Ahuja. Ahuja was a rich, handsome, and charming Sindhi, from an area that is now a province of Pakistan. That afternoon, Nanavati dropped his wife and children off at a theater production of *Tom Thumb*. He then went to his ship and got a revolver and six rounds under a false pretext. He looked for Ahuja at his office, but found he was not there. He next went to Ahuja's apartment. He got into Ahuja's bedroom and shut the door behind him. Ahuja had just come out of the bath and was combing his hair, wearing only a towel. Ahuja's servant heard several shots. When Nanavati came out less than a minute later, Ahuja was sprawled on the floor in a pool of blood.

10. Kawas Manekshaw Nanavati and his wife, Sylvia (née King), soon after their marriage in 1949. In Kawas Nanavati's trial for the murder of Sylvia's lover in 1959, the jury's acquittal helped to turn opinion against use of the jury in India.

Nanavati turned himself in and was tried for murder. He was fortunate that a fellow Parsi was the editor of a major Indian tabloid, *Blitz*. The paper campaigned relentlessly for Nanavati, comparing him to Rama, an avatar of the Hindu god Vishnu, who rescued his wife from the clutches of an evil demon king. At trial, the defense team portrayed Nanavati as a loyal husband and a patriotic hero sacrificing for his country while a rich playboy, from an outsider community, seduced his naïve wife. The defense introduced many letters to Ahuja from besotted women. Wearing a restrained white sari while testifying on behalf of her husband, Sylvia read out her own lovelorn letters to Ahuja. Nanavati claimed that he had a physical struggle with Ahuja. But the towel remained tied, undisturbed, around Ahuja's dead body. The jury acquitted by a vote of 8 to 1. Some in India thought that the jury had been overly influenced and misled by the media. The trial judge declared that the verdict was "perverse" and referred the case to the Bombay High Court. The High Court held a trial with no jury, convicted Nanavati of murder, and sentenced him to life imprisonment. *Blitz* pushed tirelessly for a pardon from the governor, which Nanavati received after spending three years in prison.

Even before the Nanavati case, Indian states had begun to curtail trial by jury. Skeptics doubted that jury trial was appropriate for a country with such deep sectarian and ethnic divides, caste and class differences, and limited formal education. They also argued that jury trial was complicated, lengthy, and expensive. Indian judges were especially concerned about the capacity of jurors. In an influential report in 1950, K. N. Wanchoo of the Allahabad High Court, later Chief Justice of India, explained that there were not "a sufficient number of the right class of people" to serve as jurors in the state. Bombay ended jury trials in 1961. Jury trial survived the longest in Calcutta (now Kolkata), but the governor abolished it in 1975, during the Emergency declared by Prime Minister Indira Gandhi. To justify declaring an emergency, the government cited external and internal threats: the recent conclusion of a war with Pakistan and nationwide strikes and protests. As with other abolitions of jury trial, a crisis provided an excuse for a step that had long been contemplated. In the case of India, this was eliminating the last of a tiny remnant. Jury trial has also been abolished in Pakistan, Malaysia, and Singapore—all former British colonies in Asia.

Jury bias in civil cases

In civil cases in the United States, juries show several forms of consistent bias, which are well documented in many studies. The biases include sympathy to individual injured plaintiffs and antipathy to corporations, especially out-of-state corporations. Plaintiffs' lawyers play on these sentiments to win large damage awards or settlements, sometimes on flimsy evidence or legal theories.

As long as they are in agreement, juries are free to let their biases run wild. Unlike judges, jurors have almost no accountability for their actions. Studies have shown that, typically, jurors will award larger damages to an injured plaintiff than judges would. Jurors are prone to the normal effect on most humans of spending other people's money on someone else, with no accountability. The problem is well illustrated by the 2009 tweet of an Arkansas civil juror: "I just gave away TWELVE MILLION DOLLARS of someone else's money!"

Allowing jurors to assess punitive damages magnifies the problem. Ordinary tort damages are "compensatory," that is, they are intended to compensate an injured plaintiff for losses. But in many cases, plaintiffs' lawyers argue for additional, "punitive" damages, which can be multiples of compensatory damages. Punitive damages are meant to punish the defendant and to deter egregious conduct. These goals allow jurors wide scope to exercise their biases.

Jury damage awards have shaped entire industries—for example, the trucking insurance industry. The number of people killed in accidents involving large trucks fell 20 percent over the decade ending in 2016. Under those circumstances, one would think that trucking insurance premiums would go down. Instead, two major insurers virtually pulled out of the market, and others raised their premiums anywhere from 10 to 30 percent. The reason is a growing number of jury verdicts in such cases with huge damage awards, including punitive damages, in the tens or even hundreds of millions of dollars.

Actual jury verdicts are not necessary for legal cases to have large economic effects. Lawyers can extract hefty settlements—and attorneys' fees—by the threat of jury trial. This is especially true in cases that have been consolidated in some fashion, either through class actions or multi-district litigation. Settlements and lawyers' fees can reach billions of dollars.

In Europe, problematic corporate behavior is handled mostly through regulation, not the civil court system. American lawyers have strenuously resisted regulation, if it means curtailment of tort liability. The lawyers prefer juries, or the threat of juries.

Supporters of the tort liability system argue that decisions by juries are more liberty-promoting than regulation. They also claim that local juries apply "community norms," which is said to be valuable in itself. It is not clear that jury verdicts in tort cases, especially with punitive damages, are liberty-promoting. Regulations impose clearer requirements, which naturally have costs. Damage awards themselves have an obvious cost, but the deterrent effects of jury verdicts are more hidden. It can be hard to know why a particular jury found liability, so the legal rule is unclear. And the amount of damages in case of liability may be wildly unpredictable. Uncertainty about rules and consequences is the opposite of the rule of law. Further, plaintiffs and plaintiffs' lawyers do not have the good of the whole public in mind. They are not interested in understanding the full range of costs and benefits, or in carefully balancing them. Generally, they simply want the maximum personal payout.

It is also not clear why local "community norms" should apply to a national or multinational corporation, especially if the damages are hundreds of millions or billions of dollars. In 1985, a Houston jury awarded Pennzoil, a company headquartered in Houston, $10.53 billion in a suit against Texaco, a company headquartered in California, for the tort of interfering with a contract. Three billion dollars of that award was punitive damages. The award forced Texaco to declare bankruptcy, the largest bankruptcy up to that time in U.S. history. Such damage awards have national and international effects. In those cases, local juries impinge on the ability of people in other places to determine the correct response. They may drain companies of funds that are needed to pay other plaintiffs. Egged on by the plaintiffs' bar, local juries can become damage hogs.

Conversely, there are parts of the United States in which juries do not award enough damages. In Northern Virginia, for example, juries have a reputation for being stingy, not awarding as much damages as a judge would to make the plaintiff whole, especially in auto accident cases. A plaintiff in such an area is stuck with a jury if the defendant makes a jury demand.

Judges have some control over jury damages. They may reduce the amount, in a procedure called remittitur. But they rarely reduce it to the level that a judge would have awarded. In the *Pennzoil v. Texaco* case, Texas courts reduced the award by $2 billion to $8.53 billion, not enough to prevent Texaco's bankruptcy. Some states allow a judge to add to the amount, called additur. That procedure is rare. Certain states have enacted caps on different types of damages, including punitive damages, but many have not. In the United States, civil jury verdicts, or the threat of them, play a significant role in the economy.

Jury deliberations: the black box

A major difficulty with the common-law jury is that it deliberates in secret and does not give reasons for what it does. Therefore it is hard to correct a jury's decision on appeal. In the past, there have been attempts to open the black box of the jury's deliberations and to decide on the propriety of what went on there. Through the mid-eighteenth century, and later in some American states, English and American judges spoke with jurors, or would allow juror statements to the court, about alleged misconduct during deliberations. Sometimes that misconduct was flipping coins or drawing straws to decide cases. Juries also gave "quotient verdicts," in which each juror came up with a number for damages and the jury averaged them. There is no reason to think that chance or quotient verdicts have disappeared.

But in the late eighteenth and early nineteenth centuries, English and American judges put severe limits on accepting juror statements about deliberations. They argued that accepting juror statements would open the door for the losing party to tamper with jurors after a verdict and would allow a single dissatisfied juror to destroy a verdict. The finality of jury verdicts would be undermined.

The refusal to accept juror statements meant rejecting much relevant evidence of juror misconduct. It came at a high cost. In 1987, the U.S. Supreme Court decided, in *Tanner v. United States*, that a trial judge was correct to reject several juror statements that the jury in that case—a complicated fraud prosecution with a trial lasting six weeks—was "on one big party." During breaks, the jurors allegedly consumed multiple mixed drinks and pitchers of beer, as well as marijuana and cocaine. Jurors described themselves as "flying." One juror expressed regret that the defendant, who was convicted, had not had a more attentive jury. A unanimous Supreme Court declared that allowing statements about such conduct would undermine "the community's trust in a system that relies on the decisions of laypeople." Shining light into the jury room, the Court worried, would destroy the institution. "It is not at all clear...that the jury system could survive such efforts to perfect it." Not only were jurors not to be held accountable for such incidents, the Court ruled; the incidents could not even be revealed.

In 2017, the Supreme Court held that the lid of the black box could be cracked open a tiny bit, but only in cases in which a juror allegedly made racially prejudiced statements. Trial judges remain concerned about the vagueness and uncertainty of this exception to the general rule.

Not all problems with jury deliberations involve flagrant misconduct; some are more subtle. Studies indicate that jury deliberations are prone to well-known group dynamics such as following a charismatic leader or compromising. Sometimes these compromises result in inconsistent verdicts. In one instance, a Virginia jury convicted a defendant of use of a firearm during an abduction, but acquitted the defendant of the abduction. Courts often uphold such inconsistent verdicts, as judges are reluctant to interfere with the jury's process of compromise—even though such a verdict is contrary to the judge's instructions and is logically inconsistent.

Trial of all issues at once

The use of lay jurors requires a continuous, concentrated trial of all issues at once. It is not fair to ask lay persons to keep coming back into court at different times to decide different issues. But professional judges can hold discontinuous proceedings, deciding each issue in a logical sequence. Discontinuous proceedings can greatly improve efficiency.

For example, in a contract case there is no need to hear evidence about damages if the court decides that there was no breach of the contract in the first place. In civil-law systems, a judge can hear evidence about breach first. If the judge decides that there was no breach, the case ends. If the judge decides there was a breach, the judge can go on to hear evidence about damages a few weeks later. But with a jury, all evidence must be presented at once, with resulting waste of time and confusion.

Length of trial

An enormous problem that has plagued jury trial is growing length. This difficulty has made jury trial unworkable in many systems. In England in the eighteenth century, when there was no plea bargaining and all felony cases went to a jury, jury trial was what we would call today a summary proceeding. Judges in the Old Bailey, the main criminal court in London, got through twelve to twenty felony trials per day, with an average in the upper teens. Many factors contributed to this speed: lack of voir dire, use of repeat juries, blunt judicial comment on the evidence, and very rapid deliberations. The adversarial system had not yet strangled jury trial.

In contrast, in the late twentieth century in Los Angeles, the average length of time for a felony trial was 7.8 trial days. In high-profile or complicated cases, the time can stretch into months. The trial of O. J. Simpson for murder took twelve months.

The problem is not limited to common-law countries. The length of trial before Japan's mixed panel has been steadily increasing. When mixed panel trials began in 2009, the average length of trial was 3.7 days, and the average time of deliberation was 6.6 hours. By 2018, those numbers were 10.8 days and 12.9 hours. The average number of witnesses questioned at trial doubled. And the number of lay judges who said that trial proceedings were "easy to understand" fell significantly. This greater length and complexity of trial may lead to expanding the practice of plea bargaining, which Japan legalized in 2018.

In Trinidad and Tobago, the length and expense of jury trials was the major factor in its massive court backlogs. A significant problem was retrials due to hung juries. Once the nation permitted non-jury trials before a judge in 2019, the backlog started to clear. One judge required only a twenty-minute trial to determine that a defendant in a case of wounding had acted in self-defense. The incident had occurred eighteen years earlier. The defendant, finally cleared, left the court in tears.

In order to be a common method of resolving cases, trial before lay jurors must be expeditious. Unless judges exert firm control over the proceedings, that will not happen. In the United States, judges increasingly impose time limits on counsel to present their case. American judges vary greatly in their willingness to impose such limits, and their length. But even the stricter judges are for the most part willing to allow the parties far more time than trial required a century ago.

Costs to jurors

One type of cost that is often downplayed or ignored is the cost to the jurors themselves. These citizens have other jobs and activities than judging cases. Many are plucked out of their ordinary life by a summons, without volunteering. The costs to them can be considerable and take different forms: time, money, stress, and even danger. Just the time, expense, and hardship of travel for jury service can be onerous. In the nineteenth century, jurors often had to travel long distances and sleep on the ground or in barns on straw. Even today, sometimes the distances jurors must travel are large, and the traffic terrible. Some juries are sequestered, that is, the jurors are isolated to avoid exposure to improper influence or information during a trial. Sequestered jurors usually stay in a hotel and are forbidden to read the newspaper, watch television, or access the internet. They may have only limited contact with others, even with each other. Sequestered jurors may be cut off from their families, friends, and colleagues for weeks.

In France and Germany, in addition to attending courtroom proceedings, prospective jurors sometimes attend various kinds of training sessions. Some departments in France, for example, take prospective jurors on a tour of a prison, so that they can see what their decision might mean for the defendant.

Some trials help to compensate for the costs to jurors with exciting or at least interesting moments. Skillful cross-examinations and closing arguments can be riveting; one of the most celebrated examples of this combination is Abraham Lincoln's cross-examination of an alleged witness of a murder and his closing argument in the case. In the 1858 Illinois case *People v. Armstrong*, Lincoln, a lawyer, represented the defendant. Under Lincoln's questioning, a witness swore insistently that he saw Armstrong strike the victim under the bright light of a moon high overhead. During his closing argument, Lincoln took out an almanac and showed that the moon was on the horizon at the time. The jury acquitted. The case is known as the Almanac Case. A talented lawyer can also make good use of demonstrative evidence, that is, pictures, models, displays, or other objects that can help the jury to understand a case. San Francisco trial lawyer Melvin Belli had a skeleton named Elmer, which he often used to show the jury how his client was injured.

But the growing length of trial imposes heavy costs on jurors. Although TV shows and movies foster the idea that trials are thrilling, most are deathly dull. As one commentator put it, "you're basically taking a 24-unit class called 'Other Peoples' Problems,' and there's no Wi-Fi." Jurors comment that trial is frustratingly slow; a juror in Washington State said, "I felt that one of the lawyers wasted days of our time. It seemed like we received lots of irrelevant information." Another complained about the "multiple side bars and delays." A side bar is when the judge confers with the lawyers out of the hearing of the jury, often to decide whether to permit a question to a witness. Some jurors must sit in trial for weeks or months of mind-numbing testimony. No wonder jurors have tried to relieve the tedium with alcohol and other substances. One jury in Australia in 2008, during a three-month trial of two men facing life sentences, got so bored listening to the 105 witnesses that five members organized a Sudoku tournament. The judge complimented the jury for being attentive and for taking copious notes. But one of the defendants, while he was testifying, noticed that jurors were writing vertically. The Sudoku tournament was revealed, and the judge ordered a mistrial. So other jurors had to listen to months of stupefying testimony all over again.

Jurors also pay a financial price. Jury service has always been, in effect, conscripted labor. In the United States in the nineteenth century, fees paid to jurors for service were only a dollar or two a day, far too low to compensate productive farmers, workers, or merchants for their loss of time. Occasional efforts were made in legislatures to raise jury fees, but these efforts seldom got far because of concern about courts' expenditure. This situation has not changed. Today in the United States in federal court jurors are paid $50 per day, less than the minimum wage. The states typically pay less; a number pay $30 per day, and several pay $5. The self-employed and many employees take a financial hit. Jurors with responsibilities for caring for children, the disabled, or the elderly face great difficulty.

Citizens of poor nations face even greater hardship having to take time off work for jury service. Relieving this onerous obligation on working-class citizens has been one of the benefits of Caribbean nations moving to non-jury trial.

There is yet another category of costs to jurors: mental hardship, cost to reputation, and danger. This category evokes the reason why so many judges and prosecutors extoll the jury system: it spares them responsibility and criticism. Many jurors find it enormously difficult to judge another human being, even collectively. A juror in Washington State felt "fright" at the "awesome responsibility to decide another man's fate," and another said that the "responsibility to place someone in jail or worse is very emotional." Some cases involve frightening or gruesome facts, which may live on in a juror's imagination for years. Some jurors are subjected to autopsy photos and detailed descriptions of bodily injuries, including torture.

Sometimes jurors are thrust into the middle of heated political controversies. For example, in 2020 a grand juror who decided on charges against the police officer who shot Breonna Taylor, a young Black emergency medical technician, in Louisville, Kentucky, made a statement through counsel: "It is patently unjust for the jurors to be subjected to the level of accountability [the prosecutor claimed they had]…simply because they received a summons to serve their community at a time when adherence to that summons forced them to be involved in a matter that has caused such a palpable division between sides." The grand juror observed that the decision of the grand jury had received intense nationwide scrutiny. "The legal system has placed the grand jurors in this matter on an island where they are left to wonder if anyone who finds them will treat them well or hold the pain and anger of the lingering questions against them." The same might be said for trial jurors who decide highly controversial cases. And digital media, including social media, now make it more difficult for jurors to disappear from public view and be forgotten after their service; they may be hounded endlessly because of their decisions.

In certain trials, such as the trial of Mexican drug cartel head Joaquín "El Chapo" Guzmán Loera in New York in 2019, the judge may order that the jurors be kept anonymous. The jurors in that case were also escorted to and from the courthouse by U.S. marshals. Sometimes elaborate transportation schemes are needed to protect jurors' anonymity and safety, as with the jurors in the trial of Kyle Rittenhouse in Kenosha, Wisconsin, in 2021 for shooting three men during protests and riots there. Even so, the judge expressed concern about a journalist who ran a red light trying to follow the jury's bus after the day's deliberations. The bus's windows were covered to safeguard the jurors' anonymity.

In some countries, it is hard to protect jurors from intimidation. In 2011, Belize abolished jury trial for murder and certain other cases. The prime minister, a lawyer, argued that for gangsters, bribing or intimidating jurors was "the easiest thing in the world." In part because of juror intimidation, other Caribbean nations permit non-jury trials for criminal cases. These include Turks and Caicos, which allowed non-jury trials in 2010, and Trinidad and Tobago in 2019.

Legal systems must cope with the weaknesses of jurors, and jurors themselves face considerable hardship. The benefits can outweigh the disadvantages, but using lay jurors effectively requires sober consideration of both.

Chapter 7
Jury control and avoidance

In order to be predictable and to enforce the law, legal systems must find ways to deal with the drawbacks of juries. This requires flexibility; rigid rules and constitutional requirements can be stumbling blocks. The need for flexibility is why Alexander Hamilton recommended against including a right to civil jury trial in the U.S. Constitution. He was concerned to accommodate "the changes which are continually happening in the affairs of society," which he thought was "a strong argument for leaving the matter to the discretion of the legislature." There are several possibilities for managing the weaknesses of juries, including limiting what cases go to a jury in the first place; controlling the inputs to the jury's decision, such as evidence and judicial instructions; requiring the jury verdict to take certain forms; reviewing the verdict on appeal; and eliminating jury trial altogether. Some countries, free from constitutional constraints, have been able to modify or abolish jury trial and to find some other means of deciding cases.

Medieval English judges did not expect a group of twelve ordinary jurors to be able to decide disputes involving complicated facts, multiple parties, multiple claims, or complex remedies. But sometimes such decisions were needed. Obviously juries could not handle all civil disputes. From early on, English kings and their judges had to figure out alternatives to resolve more complicated cases. By the late fourteenth century, the main alternative had become the Court of Chancery.

What was Chancery? It began as the king's clerical office, but evolved into a court as petitions for judgment kept pouring in. In charge was the Lord Chancellor, who until the beginning of the sixteenth century was almost always a bishop or an archbishop. This is significant, because the Chancellor ran Chancery the same way he ran his church court: using non-jury procedure that the church had developed on the continent of Europe. The procedures that the Chancellor used in Chancery, together with the substantive law that he applied, became known as equity.

Equity procedure was such an improvement on the common law and juries that Chancery quickly developed a massive substantive jurisdiction. Fraud, forgery, trusts, bankruptcy, mortgages, business associations—all were entrusted to Chancery, in many cases exclusively. Given the shortcomings of the common law, equity was vital to the functioning of the legal system in England. The jury system could not exist without strong support from non-jury adjudication. There were, in effect, two parallel systems of law in England.

That dual system spread. Many American states developed their own courts of chancery. Delaware retains a separate Court of Chancery that specializes in corporate issues. This is part of the attraction of incorporating in Delaware: adjudication by experienced, non-jury courts drawing on a detailed body of corporate law.

But, over time, both in England and the United States, many reformers wanted to merge the two systems. It seemed inefficient and expensive to maintain two separate legal systems for the same state or country. The merger of equity and the common law was done first in New York, in the Field Code of 1848. Other states, England, and the U.S. federal courts followed.

Modern American civil procedure—like equity—permits cases involving multiple parties and claims and complex factual disputes. Modern litigation often consists of extensive pre-trial procedures to discover facts (called discovery), all drawn from equity. These include document production, oral examination of witnesses or parties (called depositions), and questions that a party or witness must answer in writing (called interrogatories). But these reformers did not eliminate jury trial. In theory, this equitable discovery is tacked on the front of a jury trial—the one remaining legacy of the common law.

Summary judgment, settlement, and arbitration

In practice, that jury trial almost never happens. Pre-trial discovery is expensive and time-consuming, and if the parties engage in it they often do find relevant facts. They are reluctant to go over those facts again in an expensive jury trial, where the outcome is unpredictable. After discovery, the parties may request "summary judgment" from the judge. Under the Federal Rules of Civil Procedure, a judge may grant a party summary judgment—a decision without a jury—if "there is no genuine dispute as to any material fact." Trial judges vary widely in their willingness to grant summary judgment. They may grant summary judgment on some claims but not others. Typically, after a judge has decided motions for summary judgment, the parties soon settle the case. Often, they settle even without motions for summary judgment. Today, of civil cases reaching disposition in federal court, fewer than 1 percent are decided by jury trial. The merger of law and equity has almost killed civil jury trial.

If the settlement of civil cases were based mainly on an accurate assessment of the merits, it might not be a bad thing. But in the United States, other factors often drive settlements. Settlements take place "in the shadow of the jury," based partly on guesses about what a jury might do, which may not accurately reflect the merits. Juries are unpredictable, so a party's tolerance for risk can matter enormously. A 2016 survey of lawyers who litigate civil cases revealed that the top reasons why they settle a case, as opposed to going to jury trial, are the unpredictability of outcome and especially of damages. And very important in settlement negotiations is the expected cost of litigation to the parties, which is huge. In short, the juryless system of civil litigation we have now does not necessarily lead to more accurate, efficient outcomes. A thorough redesign would be needed for that.

Because civil litigation is so expensive and the outcomes do not necessarily reflect the merits, parties often try to avoid the courts entirely. They can do that by agreeing, in advance of a dispute or when a dispute actually begins, to have the case decided by a private person or persons. This is called arbitration. Arbitration has become a massive business around the world, with large national and international arbitration associations that can provide arbitrators (quasi-judges) and standard rules.

Diverting criminal cases from jury trial

In criminal justice, legal systems have found many ways to remove cases from jury trial.

England was an early pioneer in reclassifying crimes in order to avoid jury trial. By the time of Blackstone, Parliament was well along in its effort to classify certain criminal offenses as subject to "summary process"—decisions by justices of the peace rather than juries. Blackstone was concerned that Parliament was extending summary process so far that it might swallow jury trial, but he recognized that summary process was faster and reduced the need for jurors. Today in England some offenses are "triable either way." Sometimes in these cases, defendants are offered the choice of summary proceedings before magistrates, or jury trial with the risk of higher penalties.

One way that the Spanish legal system—and many others—has tried to mitigate the problems of lay jurors is to recharacterize particular cases as less serious, so that they are tried to judges rather than juries. Spanish prosecutors, along with prosecutors in France, Japan, and other countries, systematically undercharge crimes in order to avoid courts that use lay jurors.

Italian judges have developed a procedure, ratified by the legislature, that in effect returns to the classic inquisitorial method of judges deciding cases based on written evidence. It could be called trial on the file. For serious criminal cases, Italy uses a mixed panel of two professional judges and six lay jurors. In the late 1980s, Italy moved aggressively to remodel its criminal procedure along common-law lines. It adopted adversarial procedures. Judges were forbidden access to the investigative file during such proceedings, to make sure that they would be passive and could not intervene in the adversarial show, run by lawyers. But Italian judges rebelled. They were so devoted to the idea that they were responsible for the conduct of proceedings and the accuracy of the result that they began offering defendants a deal. Either go to adversarial trial, or accept a decision by professional judges based solely on the investigative file, with a one-third discount on the sentence. Many Italian defendants liked this idea of a trial on the file. The procedure is known as the *giudizio abbreviato* (literally "abbreviated judgment"). Italian judges have thus partly evaded trial, including trial before the mixed panel, and moved back to inquisitorial written procedure. The practice demonstrates how the judiciary can bypass efforts to introduce foreign procedures and can reduce the influence of lay jurors.

Many legal systems are moving to some form of deal to avoid the full criminal procedure, including trial before lay jurors. In part, this is because members of these systems find full investigation burdensome, and in part, they want to avoid the time and effort of adjudication by lay jurors. More defendants are now accused of white-collar financial and regulatory crimes, which are expensive to investigate and to try, with many witnesses and much expert testimony. These wealthier defendants have counsel who are more aggressive and adversarial, which drives up the cost of deciding these cases. As a result, abbreviated procedures are on the rise around the world.

One example is the German *Absprachen*, or confession bargaining. This is a deal made primarily between the presiding judge and the defense counsel, and it can be initiated by either. In return for the judge's agreement to reduce the punishment, the defendant confesses to the charge. The court then convicts the defendant in an abbreviated procedure, relying heavily on the confession. This procedure is now used for a wide range of criminal cases, including murder, and may account for as many as 50 percent of convictions for serious crime. The discount in sentence for confessing guilt is normally about one-third. In 2013, the German Constitutional Court declared that lay jurors needed to be involved in such a deal between the judiciary and the defendant. But the Court did not clarify to what extent and when.

All such efforts to get the defendant to agree to a deal are, in effect, a form of coercion. They are at odds with the idea that a judge's job in a civil-law system is to find the truth, not simply to settle a dispute between parties. A defendant is necessarily trading away full adjudication. Such deals run the risk that a defendant with a good defense is agreeing to the deal to avoid the risk of a higher sentence. This problem is even more acute in the case of common-law plea bargaining, which has now virtually replaced criminal jury trial in the United States.

The special case of plea bargaining

Plea bargaining took root in the nineteenth century in the common-law world and now has almost engulfed criminal jury trial in the United States. Common-law judges have always been more willing to view a criminal case as simply a dispute between two parties. However, in the eighteenth century, judges strenuously discouraged defendants from pleading guilty. A guilty plea cut off the possibility of hearing mitigating evidence, which might result in a lower sentence or the judge recommending a pardon.

But the growing length and expense of jury trials changed judges' attitudes to plea bargaining. English judges in the eighteenth century could get through more than a dozen felony jury trials a day. By the nineteenth century, especially in the United States, the adversarial system had begun to exert its stranglehold on the criminal trial. Jury selection, more witnesses, longer examination and cross-examination, expert testimony, rules of evidence, elaborate instructions from the judge—all slowed trial to a crawl. Judges quietly began to accept guilty pleas, first in minor cases that did not involve juries, then for more serious crimes. Unlike most of the abbreviated proceedings in civil-law countries, a plea bargain is a deal between the prosecutor and the defense. The judge has to approve the deal, but usually this is perfunctory. Plea bargains put enormous power into the hands of the prosecutor; with no real adjudication of the charges, there is little check on that official.

Until about the 1960s, the English and American legal profession either swept this practice under the rug or complained about it as an abrogation of the right to jury trial. But by then the practice had already taken firm hold. In 1952, English judge Patrick Devlin estimated that plea bargaining occurred in two-thirds of convictions. What turned the legal profession from criticism or shame-faced practice to open embrace of plea bargaining was crime. In the 1960s in the United States, violent crime skyrocketed. Murder rates in the largest American cities nearly doubled in the decade from 1960 to 1970, and robbery rates rose over 400 percent. The criminal justice system was overwhelmed. Meanwhile, the public demanded that something be done to make streets safer. Crime rates continued to rise into the 1990s.

Legislatures refused to add many more judges. Plea bargaining seemed the only way to break the logjam, to keep cases moving.

Legislatures obliged, especially in the United States, by providing more determinate sentences. Determinate, or predictable, sentences facilitate plea bargaining. Prosecutors know exactly what they are offering, and defendants know exactly what they are getting. Legislatures enacted sentencing guidelines, such as the federal Sentencing Guidelines of 1987, that made sentencing more predictable. They also enacted mandatory minimum sentences for certain offenses. Rates of plea bargaining have soared.

Today, the average discount for pleading guilty in federal court is a two-thirds reduction in the sentence. This is considerably higher than the one-third limit on sentence discount that the civil-law systems tend to impose to get defendants to agree to an abbreviated procedure. There is therefore greater coercion in the U.S. system. Although the exact numbers are hard to know, it is almost certain that some defendants with reasonable defenses are pleading guilty to avoid the risk of a much greater sentence after conviction by a jury.

In the 2010s, over 97 percent of felony convictions in federal courts in the United States were the result of a plea bargain. The rate is about 95 percent in state cases. The rate in England is somewhat lower, about 80 percent.

Nevertheless, many Americans believe that the routine way of deciding criminal cases is by jury trial. They pride themselves on this liberty, on decisions made by ordinary folks. TV shows and movies perpetuate this illusion. But Americans are no longer in a system of jury trials; they are in a system of plea bargains.

The law of evidence

For those disputes that actually went to juries, the legal system had to establish some means of control over the jury. Judges gave up imprisoning and fining jurors for perverse verdicts in *Bushell's Case* in 1670. Part of the reason why English judges were so willing to give up these methods is that they had other means of jury control.

Because common-law judges traditionally had so little power to review a jury's verdict, they focused on inputs to the jury's decision. One of those was evidence. Beginning in the late eighteenth century, common-law judges developed elaborate rules of evidence that limit the information juries hear in order to prevent them from going astray. These rules often exclude relevant evidence on the ground that it will mislead the jury. Among these rules are the "prior bad acts" rule in criminal cases, which prevents juries from hearing about prior convictions or other misdeeds of the defendant. The idea is to avoid "poisoning the well," to prevent jurors from assuming that just because a defendant did something wrong in the past, the defendant is likely to have done wrong in the current case. Another well-known rule is the "hearsay rule," which generally excludes statements about what another person said out of court. The fear is that juries will not understand that this is not the most reliable sort of evidence and that they will not be able to discount it appropriately. Each of these rules, like most rules of evidence, has exceptions and refinements.

The law of evidence is the law of jury control. In systems where professional judges traditionally decide cases or are part of a panel, rules of evidence hardly exist. Prior bad acts and hearsay chains are routinely admitted. It is understood that professional judges can discount such evidence appropriately, without needing exclusionary rules. Important constraints in those systems are the requirement of written reasons for a decision and provision for a full appeal of fact. Knowledge of prior bad acts is especially important for sentencing purposes, and civil-law systems typically decide guilt and sentence at the same time. In any case, in order to work effectively, exclusionary rules need a bifurcated court: someone to exclude the evidence (the judge) and someone from whom the evidence is excluded (the jury).

Developments in England have made clear that evidence rules are mainly needed for the jury. Now in England, almost all civil cases are decided by a judge, without a jury. In 1995, England abolished the hearsay rule in civil cases. But it has retained the hearsay rule in criminal cases, which still use juries.

Modern technological changes may be undermining traditional exclusionary rules of evidence. Jurors now have the ability to do extensive research about cases on their own, online. Although judges forbid them from doing so, just as they forbid them to read or watch news coverage of a trial in progress, the temptation for many jurors is great.

Judicial instructions on law

Besides evidence, another factor in the jury's decision is the judge's instructions on law. Judges in all common-law jurisdictions are required to state the law for the jury. A significant way of guiding the jury is to make instructions on law more detailed and elaborate. The English eighteenth-century judge Lord Mansfield was a vigorous proponent of this technique. He developed commercial law mainly by means of ever more-detailed jury instructions. In effect, Mansfield took what had previously been questions of fact for the jury and transformed them into questions of law for the judge.

Later English and American judges enthusiastically applied this technique. A classic example is the English case of *Hadley v. Baxendale* (1854), concerning damages for a breach of contract. Hadley owned a flour mill whose crankshaft broke. Hadley contracted with Baxendale to deliver the broken crankshaft to engineers by a certain date for repair, but Baxendale delivered it late, and Hadley lost business as a result. The jury awarded lost profits to Hadley as damages, and Baxendale appealed. Before that case, it was entirely up to the jury to decide the amount of damages. But *Hadley* laid down the rule that damages for breach of contract were limited to circumstances that were reasonably foreseeable to the parties at the time they made the contract. According to the court, loss of such business was not reasonably foreseeable to Baxendale unless Hadley had told him at the time of contracting that that would happen (which he had not done). The court awarded a new trial in order for the trial judge to give this instruction to the jury. More detailed instructions thus had the effect of clarifying the law and making it more predictable. Today, many English judges carefully guide criminal juries with an elaborate decision tree, tailored to each case, called a "route to verdict."

However, a problem with detailed instructions on law is that the jury may nullify them or not be able to understand them. Despite judges' efforts to refine and develop the law, with jury verdicts we may remain in an era of rough justice.

Judicial comment on evidence

The most powerful and enduring tool that English judges had to control verdicts was summing up and commenting on evidence to the jury. Judges could and did give their opinion of how a case should be decided, and sometimes used strong language in doing so. In most cases, jurors were grateful for the judge's guidance.

English judges routinely gave juries their opinion about the evidence in both civil and criminal cases. Writing in the late seventeenth century, the prominent English judge Sir Matthew Hale explained that judicial comment on evidence was a vital aid to jury trial. He wrote that a judge not only directed the jurors on matters of law, but the practice of comment allowed the judge "in matters of fact, to give them a great light and assistance by his weighing the evidence before them, and observing where the question and knot of the business lies, and by showing them his opinion even in matter of fact, which is a great advantage and light to lay men." A study of a judge's notebooks from the 1750s concluded that the judge dominated jury verdicts. Trial judges often recommended that the jury find for one party or the other, and juries usually complied.

English judges' power to comment on evidence eventually caused the demise of the civil jury there. As English judges already dominated juries, it was a small additional step to eliminate civil juries and to save the trouble and expense. That process began in the mid-nineteenth century and was virtually complete in the mid-twentieth century. The English legal profession had confidence that English judges were on the whole impartial and competent. In 1850, *The Times* of London declared that in 99 cases out of 100, the verdict turned more on the judge than the jury. The "mere pantomimical expression of disgust or incredulity on the part of the presiding magistrate will be sufficient to neutralize the hypothesis of an advocate, or to shake the testimony of a witness."

In criminal cases today, English judges are less likely to comment directly on the evidence than previously. But they are required to sum up the evidence for the jury. The same is true of Australian and New Zealand judges. This is viewed as an essential corrective to two conflicting arguments from the prosecution and the defense, which may prove confusing to the jury.

This is not so in American courtrooms. The power of American judges to comment on evidence or to sum up the evidence has been, in effect, abolished. How did this happen? Through the late nineteenth century, federal courts and those of some states retained the English practice of the judge commenting on evidence to the jury, sometimes robustly. As long as the trial judge separated the law from the facts and made it clear that the facts were for the jury to decide, appellate courts allowed strong judicial comment.

But gradually, over the course of the nineteenth century, states began to curtail this judicial power. One concern was the bias of trial judges, who now were elected in many of the states. Another was the power of the American legal profession, which resented judicial interference with its emotional rhetoric. As appeals developed in common-law systems, appellate courts began to trim the power of the trial judge over the jury; they reversed trial judges who commented on the evidence. Trial judges increasingly refrained from thorough summing-up or comments, and juries were left to cope with the evidence and arguments of counsel without guidance. The trial judge operated as less of a check on the adversarial system, with resulting jury confusion and susceptibility to lawyers' rhetoric.

As judicial comment withered, prominent legal scholars claimed that the only way to save jury trial from terminal decline was to revive the power of trial judges to comment on evidence. In 1923, John Henry Wigmore, author of the leading treatise on evidence, wrote that the loss of judicial power to comment on evidence "has done more than any other one thing to impair the general efficiency of jury trial as an instrument of justice." If the power were restored, he predicted, a "new birth of long life will then be open for the great and beneficent institution of Trial by Jury."

Requiring the jury to answer specific questions

Judges can try to control what the jury hears, but they cannot penetrate the black box of jury deliberations, and so understand definitively the jury's decision. One way to get more information about how juries are deciding cases, and to guide how they decide them, is to require them to answer specific questions as part of their verdict.

In common-law countries, there are three main forms of jury verdict. These vary in how much they guide or control jurors. The least restrictive is the simple binary guilty-or-not-guilty, liable-or-not-liable verdict, which is called a general verdict. The most restrictive is the special verdict, which asks a jury specific questions about the facts but does not ask for a general conclusion. The judge provides that, based on the jury's answers to the specific questions. Yet a third type of verdict is a hybrid:

the general verdict with interrogatories, in which the jury gives a general verdict but also answers specific questions.

In common-law countries, a general verdict is normally used in criminal cases, which makes it easier for juries to nullify the law. Special verdicts are rarely used, in either criminal or civil cases. But studies have shown that jurors are more apt to focus on the law and evidence during deliberations if they are asked specific questions. Today in the United States, in the rare civil trials that occur, a general verdict with interrogatories is common. In the 2012 patent infringement case of *Apple v. Samsung*, tried before a jury in northern California, the verdict form consisted of 19 pages densely packed with questions.

Civil-law countries, which have such a strong tradition of reasoned judgments, have taken the desire for specific questions even further. Some of them do not hesitate to ask juries detailed questions in criminal cases. When these systems use independent juries, rather than mixed panels, judges are especially anxious, and pile on questions. This practice began in France in the late eighteenth century, with the advent of independent juries. French juries tended to be confused by all the questions. Nevertheless, from there the practice of asking detailed questions of independent juries spread throughout Europe. In one Russian trial in the 1990s, the judge submitted 1,047 questions to the jury.

One of the most spectacular examples is Spain, which uses an independent jury, not a mixed panel. Spain not only asks detailed questions of the jury, but also requires a jury to give written reasons for its decisions, with reference to the evidence. An illustration of what can happen when lay jurors try to give reasons is the trial of the Basque separatist Mikel Otegi in 1997. Otegi shot two Spanish police officers at point-blank range with a shotgun. In that case, the judge asked the jury 95 questions about the shootings. The jury acquitted Otegi, shocking the Spanish public and prompting calls for the repeal of the jury system, or suspension of it in the Basque Country. When it came to giving reasons, the jury was very succinct. It commented that the main charges were "deficiently proved" and that it "had doubts." The Spanish Supreme Court overturned this verdict, on the grounds that the jury did not give adequate reasons for its decision. The Otegi case demonstrates the attachment of Spanish courts to reasoned, written decisions, which they try to get even though they are using independent lay juries. And the case illustrates the pervasive disgust with jury nullification among judges in civil-law countries.

The concern with independent juries acting incompetently or lawlessly is a major reason why so many civil-law systems—including France, Germany, and Italy—have switched from the use of independent, all-lay juries to the mixed panel.

In some systems, even mixed panels must give written reasons for their decisions. In Germany, the maxim is *kein Urteil ohne Gründe*: no judgment without reasons. So seriously does the German system take this maxim that the mixed panels of lay jurors and professional judges must provide a written opinion. If a professional judge is in the majority, the judge writes the opinion; if not, a court clerk helps the lay jurors write it. The Italian and Japanese mixed panels also produce written decisions. Written reasons are more satisfying for the litigants, to know that their positions have been considered. And written reasons encourage decision-makers to carefully evaluate the facts and law. They facilitate full appeal.

Appeal

Once a jury has made its decision and handed in its verdict, the question of whether to correct it arises. The civil-law systems typically provide for a very thorough appeal. This appeal focuses not on procedural mistakes (such as whether this or that piece of evidence should have been admitted), but on the merits of the case (whether the defendant is guilty). The appellate court reviews the work of the court that first hears the case for accuracy of both fact and law, with no presumption that that decision is correct. This is known as appeal de novo (starting from the beginning) of both fact and law. Germany, Italy, and Japan have this full appeal of the decisions of the mixed panels.

Such a thorough appeal on the merits has always been thought to be incompatible with trial by an independent lay jury. The jury verdict is inscrutable. Jury deliberations occur in secret, and juries usually give no official reasons for what they do. Without the jurors giving reasons, it can be hard to evaluate their work. And if a system is willing to tolerate jury nullification, a thorough review is counterproductive. The common-law rule about double jeopardy prevents the prosecution from appealing in a criminal case. This permits nullification by acquittal. Civil-law systems allow the prosecution to appeal as well as the defense, and therefore put a check on nullification.

The oral proceedings at a common-law trial, without a written opinion, are more difficult to review. A lengthy trial transcript is harder to review than an organized investigative file. And the common-law systems tend to put a heavy emphasis on "demeanor evidence," that is, the way a witness sounds, looks, or acts when giving testimony. This emphasis on demeanor evidence persists today despite numerous studies showing that it can be deeply misleading. Demeanor evidence can be difficult for an appellate court to review, even with a video recording, and impossible to review without one.

As a result, common-law systems resisted appeal for a long time. There was no appeal as of right whatsoever in criminal cases until 1907 in England and 1889 in the U.S. federal courts. The American states allowed appeal in criminal cases somewhat earlier in the nineteenth century. And there were, in effect, mechanisms for appeal of civil verdicts earlier.

But the appeal allowed is rarely on the merits. Typically, it concerns procedural questions, not the merits of the case. Was this piece of evidence improperly admitted? Was the judge's instruction correct? Not: is the defendant guilty? Because review of the jury's conclusion—the verdict—is so difficult, the common-law systems mainly review what the jury hears. And the form that correction of error often takes is granting a new trial.

New trial as a method of jury control has the benefit of seeming to preserve jury power, as the judge simply hands the case to another jury. But it is an expensive method, as the whole case has to be tried over again, with no guarantee of a correct result the next time. The court does not simply enter judgment for the correct party. This remedy became a significant contributor to the inefficiency of jury trial. In 1906 in St. Paul, Minnesota, law professor Roscoe Pound declared in an address to the American Bar Association's annual meeting that the "lavish" granting of new trials was "the worst feature of American procedure." He claimed that, at that time, over 40 percent of state appellate decisions resulted in a new trial.

Abolition of the jury

Countries that do not have constitutional rights to jury trial, or are able to amend their constitutions more easily, can adjust their systems to provide more accurate, efficient ways to decide cases. Many systems, including France, Germany, and Italy, have switched from an all-lay jury to a mixed panel of professional judges and lay jurors. Supporters of the all-lay jury point out that these systems switched at times of great political stress, during the Vichy regime, the Weimar Republic, and the rise of fascism in Italy. But in these countries, the all-lay jury had long been under attack. And these systems have stuck with the mixed panel during far more stable times. Japan's adoption of the mixed panel in 2009 shows the practice's appeal. The mixed panel answers the call for lay participation in a more workable way. Indeed, arguably these systems allow for more lay participation in serious criminal cases than the United States does.

Other systems that once used lay jurors have found it preferable to adjudicate without them. These include India, Malaysia, and Singapore. Trinidad and Tobago, Belize, and Turks and Caicos are moving away from criminal juries to adjudication by judges. In the common-law world, civil juries have virtually disappeared. England has almost abolished them, as has Australia, New Zealand, and Canada. Civil juries proved to be not worth the time, effort, and expense. Meanwhile the United States limps along, in theory providing jury trial in a wide range of criminal and civil cases, but in practice vanishingly few.

Chapter 8
The future of the jury

Given the difficulties of reconciling lay participation with a modern legal system, one may well wonder about the outlook for the jury. Legal systems in common-law countries and elsewhere have sidelined the independent jury, especially through plea bargaining. For cases that actually go to trial, getting jurors to show up is hard, and jury trials have become exasperatingly long, tedious, and confusing. Even mixed panels are succumbing to the disease of lengthening trial. And legal systems are also bypassing mixed panels, through undercharging and various forms of deals.

There are many possibilities for jury reform, targeted to different problems with the system. In the United States, for example, concern has grown about whether juries are truly representative of the community. As a result, academics and some judges have advocated abolishing peremptory challenges. In 2021, the Supreme Court of Arizona took that step. England and Wales, with its strong emphasis on random selection of jurors, is a potential model for reformers interested in this problem. Argentine-style quotas based on sex or other characteristics are also a possibility.

The mixed panel of professional judges and lay jurors has proved to be attractive around the world. The lay jurors on mixed panels have shown that they sometimes do affect the outcome of cases, particularly the sentence. Mixed panels provide for lay participation, while at the same time promoting understanding of and attention to the law. They are a possible pattern for reform in both common-law and civil-law countries.

Time limits on presentation of evidence and arguments at trial appear to be increasingly necessary. Many judges in the United States currently set time limits on the parties, sometimes enforced by a court clerk keeping a chess clock.

Some of the most novel proposals for reform concern technology. Technology, in the form of remote communication, may grant new life to lay participation. In the United States, certain constitutional rules, such as the requirement of unanimity, limit experimentation with juries. But other countries have more opportunities to innovate. How legal systems use technology will depend on the purposes of lay jurors.

If the desired purpose is to secure the decision of a representative group of citizens, remote communication can help to assemble much larger, more representative groups of jurors that can hear evidence streamed to them. We could almost be back in the era of Athenian-size juries. Panels of fifty or more would be possible. To hold jurors' attention and to reduce the cost to them, presentations of evidence would have to be much snappier. In straightforward cases, trials could be limited to two hours total presentation time, with an hour for each side. These could be done live or could be recorded in advance, under the guidance of a judge. For more complicated cases, presentations could occur in one-hour daily segments. Jurors could go on with their normal lives while serving. Care would need to be taken to make sure that jurors were paying attention and that they had the appropriate technology. In the COVID era, some courts have started supplying devices to jurors. If the presentations are recorded, jurors could have the advantage of replaying testimony or arguments. Deliberations would look different, and could even be eliminated, as in ancient Athens, in favor of direct voting. With larger juries, unanimity could not be required; most likely, some sort of super-majority rule would exist, as in many systems already today. Court experience during COVID has shown that, using remote technology, a wider cross-section of the population is likely to participate, including racial minorities, the self-employed, the young, and the old.

If the desired purpose of lay participation is to benefit the lawyers by allowing them to tailor the panel more to their liking, remote technology can help with that too. Many lawyers and judges have already been pleased with the results of remote jury selection during COVID. Lawyers and trial consultants report that, when jurors respond from their own homes, they are more likely to be forthcoming in answers to questions on voir dire. This appears to be because they are more comfortable in familiar surroundings. During online jury selection, potential jurors have been shown eating in bed, riding an exercise bike, and grooming pets. They are more unguarded at such moments, which suits the lawyers. Lawyers and trial consultants also have a better opportunity to observe the surroundings and activities of the juror and to make better guesses about likely sympathies and antipathies.

And if the desired purpose is to secure greater expertise, in the form of special panels, remote technology can also help. With no travel costs, experts could be assembled from anywhere in the country or the world. They could watch streamlined presentations, review data, ask and answer questions, and consult with each other. They could be paid an appropriate amount and not have to waste time. Patent and other technical cases could benefit enormously from such expert jurors.

These are a few of the possibilities. With the spread of democracy and the idea of self-rule, popular desire for lay participation in legal systems will endure. A clear-eyed and open-minded search for effective ways to include jurors can make this aspiration a reality.

References

Introduction

Jurors' oath: *Benchbook for U.S. District Court Judges*, 6th ed. (Washington, DC: Federal Judicial Center, 2013), 269.

Alexis de Tocqueville, *Democracy in America*, ed. J. P. Mayer, trans. George Lawrence (New York: Harper Perennial, 1988) (1835), 271.

Chapter 1

Plato, Apology of Socrates (*c.*399 BCE), in *Four Texts on Socrates*, ed. and trans. Thomas G. West and Grace Starry West (Ithaca, NY: Cornell University Press, rev. ed., 1998), 89 (35b–c).

Athenian law of 410 BCE, quoted in Daniela Cammack, "Plato and Athenian Justice," *History of Political Thought* 36, no. 4 (Winter 2015): 625–6.

Assize of Clarendon (1166), in *English Historical Documents: 1042–1189*, ed. D. C. Douglas and G. W. Greenaway, 2nd ed. (London: Eyre & Spottiswoode, 1981), 2:440–3.

Henry de Bracton, *On the Laws and Customs of England*, ed. and trans. Samuel E. Thorne (Cambridge, MA: Harvard University Press, 1968) (*c.*1230s–1250s), 2:328.

Magna Carta (1215), translation in Faith Thompson, *Magna Carta: Its Role in the Making of the English Constitution 1300–1629* (Minneapolis: University of Minnesota Press, 1948), 68.

Petition of Right (1628), in *Sources of English Constitutional History*, ed. and trans. Carl Stephenson and Frederick George Marcham (New York: Harper & Row, rev. ed., 1972), 1:451.

Barbara W. Tuchman, *A Distant Mirror: The Calamitous 14th Century* (New York: Ballantine Books, 1978), 92–3.

John Fortescue, *On the Laws and Governance of England*, ed. and trans. S. B. Chrimes (Cambridge: Cambridge University Press, 1942) (*c.*1470), 38–40.

Chapter 2

Chief Justice William Scroggs in the Popish Plot trials, quoted in John H. Langbein, Renée Lettow Lerner, and Bruce P. Smith, *History of the Common Law: The Development of Anglo-American Legal Institutions* (New York: Aspen Publishers, 2009), 655.

William Blackstone, *Commentaries on the Laws of England* (Chicago: University of Chicago Press, 1979) (1768) 3:379.

Brutus, Essay XV (March 20, 1788), in *The Anti-Federalist: Writings by the Opponents of the Constitution*, ed. Herbert J. Storing (Chicago: University of Chicago Press, 1985), 183.

Alexander Hamilton, The Federalist No. 78 (May 28, 1788), in *The Federalist*, ed. George W. Carey and James McClellan (Indianapolis: Liberty Fund, 2001), 402–3.

Alexander Hamilton, The Federalist No. 83 (July 5, 9, and 12, 1788), 432–3. Blackstone, *Commentaries*, 3:379–80.

"Mr. General Motors": *General Motors Corp. v. Jackson*, 636 So. 2d 310, 344 (Miss. 1994) (Chief Justice Armis Hawkins, dissenting).

Tocqueville on the jury as a political institution: Tocqueville, *Democracy in America*, 273–4.

On Indian protests against curtailment of jury trial, see Mitra Sharafi, *Law and Identity in Colonial South Asia* (Cambridge: Cambridge University Press, 2014), 204–5.

Tocqueville on the jury as a school for democracy: Tocqueville, *Democracy in America*, 274–5.

Effects of jury service on civic engagement: John Gastil, E. Pierre Deess, Philip J. Weiser, and Cindy Simmons, *The Jury and Democracy: How Jury Deliberation Promotes Civic Engagement and Political Participation* (New York: Oxford University Press, 2010), 48, 113.

Quotations from jurors: Gastil et al., *The Jury and Democracy*, 74, 94.

On the benefit of juries to judges: Charles de Secondat, baron de Montesquieu, *The Spirit of the Laws*, ed. and trans. Anne M. Cohler, Basia Carolyn Miller, and Harold Samuel Stone

(Cambridge: Cambridge University Press, 1989) (1748), 158.
Thomas More, quoted in William Roper, *The Lyfe of Sir Thomas Moore, knighte*, ed. Elsie Vaughan Hitchcock (London: Early English Text Society by Humphrey Milford, 1935) (*c*.1557), 45; Thomas More, "The Debellation of Salem and Bizance" (1533), in *Complete Works of St. Thomas More*, ed. John Guy, Ralph Keen, Clarence Miller, and Ruth McGugan (New Haven: Yale University Press, 1987), 10:95; Matthew Hale, *History of the Pleas of the Crown* (London: E. and R. Nutt, and R. Gosling, for F. Gyles, T. Woodward, and C. Davis, 1736) (*c*.1675), 2:313; James Fitzjames Stephen, *History of the Criminal Law of England* (London: MacMillan and Co., 1883), 1:573.

Use of grand juries to deflect attention from prosecutors: Motion by grand juror for release of grand jury transcripts in *Kentucky v. Hankison*, Sept. 28, 2020, 4–5, at https://interactive.whas11.com/pdfs/scannedmotiongjrelease.pdf.

Cost of the tort system: Renée Lettow Lerner, book review of Amalia D. Kessler, *Inventing American Exceptionalism: The Origins of American Adversarial Legal Culture, 1800–1877*, in *Journal of Legal Education* 67 (2018): 889.

Chapter 3

Quote from Learned Hand: U.S. *ex rel. McCann v. Adams*, 126 F.2d 774, 776 (2d Cir. 1942).

Bushell's Case, Vaughan 135, 136, 124 Eng. Rep. 1006 (C.P. 1670).

On the trial of John Peter Zenger: Gouverneur Morris, quoted in William H. Adams, *Gouverneur Morris, An Independent Life* (New Haven: Yale University Press, 2003), 11. James Alexander, "A Brief Narrative of the Case and Trial of John Peter Zenger" (1736), in Stanley N. Katz, ed., *The Case and Trial of John Peter Zenger* (Cambridge, MA: Harvard University Press, 1989), 101.

Resolves of the Stamp Act Congress, October 1765, in C. A. Weslager, *The Stamp Act Congress: With an Exact Copy of the Complete Journal* (Newark: University of Delaware Press, 1976), 126.

Declaration of Independence, July 4, 1776, at https://www.archives.gov/founding-docs/declaration-transcript.

Horace Gray on juries and revolutionaries: Josiah Quincy, Samuel Miller Quincy, and Horace Gray, *Reports of Cases Argued and*

Adjudged in the Superior Court of Judicature of the Province of Massachusetts (Boston: Little, Brown, 1865), 571–2.

1857 English case on jury attitudes toward railroads: *Toomey v. London, Brighton & S. Coast*. Ry. Co, 140 Eng. Rep. 694, 696 (C.P. 1857).

Sparf & Hansen v. U.S., 156 U.S. 51, 103 (1895).

"A sabotage of justice" and a 1990 letter from a juror in Washington, DC: Randall Kennedy, "The Angry Juror," *Wall Street Journal*, Sept. 30, 1994, at A12.

Chapter 4

Patrick Devlin on English juries: Patrick, Lord Devlin, *Trial by Jury* (London: Stevens & Sons, rev. ed., 1966), 20.

Napoleon on the French jury: Napoléon Bonaparte, quoted in James M. Donovan, *Juries and the Transformation of Criminal Justice in France in the Nineteenth & Twentieth Centuries* (Chapel Hill: University of North Carolina Press, 2010), 43.

North Carolina pamphlet on women on juries: quoted in Linda L. Kerber, *No Constitutional Right to Be Ladies: Women and Obligations of Citizenship* (New York: Hill and Wang, 1998), 139.

"Woman is still regarded as the center of home and family life." *Hoyt v. Florida*, 368 U.S. 57, 62 (1961).

The key-man system and 1967 survey: Charles A. Lindquist, "An Analysis of Juror Selection Procedures in the United States District Courts," *Temple Law Quarterly* 41 (1967): 32, 44.

Fair cross-section requirement: *Thiel v. Southern Pacific Co.*, 328 U.S. 217, 223–4 (1946).

Frederick Douglass, *Life and Times of Frederick Douglass, Written by Himself* (Boston: De Wolfe & Fiske Co., 1892), 460.

The Colored Tribune: "Our Jury Commissioners," *Colored Tribune* (Savannah, GA), June 3, 1876, at 2, quoted in James Forman, Jr., "Juries and Race in the Nineteenth Century," *Yale Law Journal* 113 (2004): 895, 931.

Avery v. Georgia, 345 U.S. 559, 562 (1953).

Mark Twain [Samuel Clemens], *Roughing It* (New York: Oxford University Press, 1996) (1872), 92–3. Mark Twain [Samuel Clemens], "Americans and the English," address, July 4, 1873, London, in *Great Speeches by Mark Twain*, ed. Bob Blaisdell (Mineola, NY: Dover, 2013), 7–8.

Voir dire in the Terry Nichols case: "American Jury Voir Dire Questioning in the Nichols Case," ed. David Schermbrucker, *Criminal Lawyers' Association Newsletter* (Toronto, Ontario) 18, no. 6 (December 1997): 11.

Chapter 5

U.S. Constitution, Amendment VI, at https://constitutioncenter.org/ interactive-constitution/full-text.

Duncan v. Louisiana, 391 U.S. 145 (1968).

On the number twelve destroying individual accountability: James Stephen, *History of the Criminal Law of England*, 568.

Report of the Debates and Proceedings of the Convention for the Revision of the Constitution of the State of New York, reported by William G. Bishop and William H. Attree (Albany, NY: printed at the office of the Evening Atlas, 1846), 111 (remarks of Mr. Hunt).

Williams v. Florida, 399 U.S. 78, 88–9 (1970).

Edward Coke, "The First Part of the Institutes of the Lawes of England" (1628), in *The Selected Writings and Speeches of Sir Edward Coke*, ed. Steve Shepherd (Indianapolis: Liberty Fund, 2003), 2:728 (227b).

On the deprivation of jurors and the case of the tempest of 1499: David J. Seipp, "Jurors, Evidences and the Tempest of 1499," in *The Dearest Birthright of the People of England: The Jury in the History of the Common Law*, ed. John Cairns and Grant McLeod (London: Bloomsbury Publishing, 2002), 75–92.

Alexander Pope, "The Rape of the Lock" (1714), in *"The Rape of the Lock" and Other Poems*, ed. Thomas Marc Parrott (Boston: Ginn, 1906), 14 (canto III, line 22).

Chapter 6

Alexander Hamilton, *The Federalist* No. 83, 433.

On the need to reduce cases to a simple point to be decided by a jury: Montesquieu, *Spirit of the Laws*, 76–7. Alexander Hamilton, *The Federalist* No. 83, 438.

The understanding of jurors: John Adams, "Diary Notes on the Rights of Juries," Feb. 12, 1771, in *Legal Papers of John Adams*, ed. L. Kinvin Wroth and Hiller B. Zobel (Cambridge, MA: Harvard University Press, 1965), 1:229–30.

Blackstone, *Commentaries*, 3:379.

Gilbert Abbott à Beckett, *The Comic Blackstone* (Union, NJ: Lawbook Exchange, 2000) (1846), 275.

Lewis Carroll, *Alice's Adventures in Wonderland* (London: Macmillan, 1995) (1865), 164–5.

W. S. Gilbert, *Trial by Jury*, libretto (1875), at https://gsarchive.net/trial/tbj_lib.pdf, 1–2, 16.

On Alfred the Great's invention: Mark Twain, *Roughing It*, 92. "Trial by Jury," *New York Times*, June 1, 1871.

"Globe Sights" from the *Atchison* (KS) *Globe*, Jan. 27, 1904, 4, col. 2.

Justice Robert Grier: *Goodyear v. Day*, 10 F. Cas. 678, 683 (C.C.D.N.J. 1852).

Interviews with jurors in the Casey Anthony case: David Tunno, *Fixing the Engine of Justice: Diagnosis and Repair of Our Jury System* (Bloomington, IN: iUniverse, 2013), 32.

Remarks of Chief Justice Ivor Archie of Trinidad and Tobago: "Twelve Clueless Men: A Drive to Abolish Jury Trials," *The Economist*, Aug. 30, 2014.

U.S. Supreme Court on emotional susceptibility of jurors: *Pleasants v. Fant*, 89 U.S. (22 Wall.) 116, 121 (1874).

Jerome Frank, *Courts on Trial: Myth and Reality in American Justice* (Princeton: Princeton University Press, 1949), 130.

Judge Thomas Ruffin on advocates: *State v. Moses*, 13 N.C. 452, 458 (1830).

Juries as "the safeguard of brigands": members of the French national legislature, quoted in Dovovan, *Juries and the Transformation of Criminal Justice in France*, 40.

Mohandas Karamchand (Mahatma) Gandhi, "Trials by Jury," *Young India*, Aug. 27, 1931, 240.

Quotation of K. N. Wanchoo: Report of the Uttar Pradesh Judicial Reforms Committee, 1950–51, (Allahabad, 1952), 1:54–5, quoted in James Jaffe, "'Not the Right People': Why Jury Trials Were Abolished in India," *Socio-Legal Review*, Oct. 1, 2020, at https://www.sociolegalreview.com/post/not-the-right-people-why-jury-trials-were-abolished-in-india.

2009 tweet of Arkansas juror: David Chartier, "Juror's Twitter posts cited in motion for mistrial," *Ars Technica*, March 15, 2009, https://arstechnica.com/information-technology/2009/03/jurors-twitter-posts-cited-in-motion-for-mistrial/.

Tanner v. United States, 483 U.S. 107, 115–16, 120–1 (1987).

The jury taking a 24-unit class called "Other Peoples' Problems": Jeff
   Bennion, Eric Yosomono, and Gregory Myers, "5 Stupid Juries
   That Prove the Justice System Is Broken," *Cracked*, July 18, 2013,
   at https://www.cracked.com/article_20366_5-stupid-juries-that-
   prove-justice-system-broken.html.
Quotations from jurors about slowness of trial and time-wasting: Gastil
   et al., *The Jury and Democracy*, 79, 90. On heavy responsibility of
   jurors: ibid., 88.
Motion by grand juror for release of grand jury transcripts in
   Kentucky v. Hankison, Sept. 28, 2020, 6, 9, at https://interactive.
   whas11.com/pdfs/scannedmotiongjrelease.pdf.
Dean Barrow, prime minister of Belize, quoted in "Twelve Clueless
   Men: A Drive to Abolish Jury Trials," *The Economist*,
   Aug. 30, 2014.

Chapter 7

Alexander Hamilton, *The Federalist* No. 83, 441.
Matthew Hale, *The History of the Common Law of England*, ed.
   Charles M. Gray (Chicago: University of Chicago Press, 1971)
   (first published posthumously 1713), 164–5.
Judicial comment leading to the demise of the civil jury in England:
   The Times (of London), March 29, 1850, at 4, col. D, quoted in
   Conor Hanly, "The Decline of Civil Jury Trial in Nineteenth
   Century England," *Journal of Legal History* 26 (2005): 259.
Wigmore on judicial comment in the United States: John
   H. Wigmore, *A Treatise on the Anglo-American System of
   Evidence in Trials at Common Law*, 2nd ed. (Boston: Little,
   Brown, 1923), 5:557.
Otegi case in Spain: verdict translated and printed in Stephen
   C. Thaman, *Comparative Criminal Procedure: A Casebook
   Approach*, 2nd ed. (Durham, NC: Carolina Academic Press,
   2008), 198.
Roscoe Pound's 1906 address to the American Bar Association: Roscoe
   Pound, "The Causes of Popular Dissatisfaction with the
   Administration of Justice," reprinted in *Journal of the American
   Judicature Society* 20 (1937): 178.

Further reading

Ancient juries

Aristophanes. *The Wasps.* (422 BCE) In *Aristophanes: Clouds, Wasps, Peace.* Edited and translated by Jeffrey Henderson. Cambridge, MA: Harvard University Press, 1998. (Loeb Classical Library.)

Cammack, Daniela. "Plato and Athenian Justice." *History of Political Thought* 36 (2015): 611–42.

Cammack, Daniela. "The Popular Courts in Athenian Democracy." *Journal of Politics* 84, no.4 (October 2022): 1997–2010. https://doi.org/10.1086/719417.

Lanni, Adriaan. *Law and Justice in the Courts of Classical Athens.* Cambridge: Cambridge University Press, 2006.

Plato. Apology of Socrates. (*c.*399 BCE) In *Four Texts on Socrates.* Translated and edited by Thomas G. West and Grace Starry West. Ithaca, NY: Cornell University Press, rev. ed., 1998.

Juries in England

Baker, John. *An Introduction to English Legal History.* 5th ed. Oxford: Oxford University Press, 2019.

Blackstone, William. *Commentaries on the Laws of England.* Vol. 3. Chicago: University of Chicago Press, 1979.

Brand, Paul, and Joshua Getzler, eds. *Judges and Judging in the History of the Common Law and Civil Law.* Cambridge: Cambridge University Press, 2012.

Cairns, John, and Grant McLeod, eds. *The Dearest Birthright of the People of England: The Jury in the History of the Common Law.* London: Bloomsbury, 2002.

Cockburn, J. S. and Thomas A. Green, eds. *Twelve Good Men and True: The Criminal Trial Jury in England, 1200–1800*. Princeton, NJ: Princeton University Press, 1988.

Dawson, John P. *A History of Lay Judges*. Cambridge, MA: Harvard University Press, 1960.

Devlin, Patrick. *Trial by Jury*. London: Stevens & Sons, rev. ed., 1966.

Green, Thomas Andrew. *Verdict According to Conscience: Perspectives on the English Criminal Trial Jury 1200–1800*. Chicago: University of Chicago Press, 1985.

Hanly, Conor. "The Decline of Civil Jury Trial in Nineteenth Century England." *Journal of Legal History* 26 (2005): 253–78.

Langbein, John H. *The Origins of Adversary Criminal Trial*. New York: Oxford University Press, 2003.

Langbein, John H., Renée Lettow Lerner, and Bruce P. Smith. *History of the Common Law: The Development of Anglo-American Legal Institutions*. New York: Aspen, 2009.

Oldham, James. *English Common Law in the Age of Mansfield*. Chapel Hill: University of North Carolina Press, 2004.

Seipp, David J. "Jurors, Evidences and the Tempest of 1499." In John Cairns and Grant McLeod, eds, *The Dearest Birthright of the People of England: The Jury in the History of the Common Law*. London: Bloomsbury, 2002, 75–92.

Stephen, James Fitzjames. *History of the Criminal Law of England*. London: Macmillan, 1883.

Juries in the United States

Abramson, Jeffrey. *We, the Jury: The Jury System and the Ideal of Democracy*. New York: Basic Books, 1994.

Adler, Stephen J. *The Jury: Trial and Error in the American Courtroom*. New York: Times Books, 1994.

Amar, Akhil Reed. *The Bill of Rights: Creation and Reconstruction*. New Haven: Yale University Press, 1998.

Appleman, Laura I. *Defending the Jury: Crime, Community, and the Constitution*. New York: Cambridge University Press, 2015.

Bibas, Stephanos. *The Machinery of Criminal Justice*. New York: Oxford University Press, 2012.

Bornstein, Brian H., and Edie Greene. *The Jury Under Fire: Myth, Controversy, and Reform*. New York: Oxford University Press, 2017.

Burns, Robert P. *The Death of the American Trial*. Chicago: University of Chicago Press, 2009.

Conrad, Clay S. *Jury Nullification: The Evolution of a Doctrine.*
Washington, DC: Cato Institute Press, 2014.

Devine, Dennis J. *Jury Decision Making: The State of the Science.*
New York: New York University Press, 2012.

Diamond, Shari Seidman, and Mary R. Rose. "The Contemporary
American Jury." *Annual Review of Law and Social Science* 14
(2018): 239–58.

Fairfax, Roger A., Jr., ed. *Grand Jury 2.0: Modern Perspectives on the
Grand Jury.* Durham, NC: Carolina Academic Press, 2010.

Forman, James, Jr. "Juries and Race in the Nineteenth Century." *Yale
Law Journal* 113 (2004): 895–938.

Frank, Jerome. *Courts on Trial: Myth and Reality in American
Justice.* Princeton: Princeton University Press, 1949.

Friedman, Lawrence M. *A History of American Law.* 4th ed.
New York: Oxford University Press, 2019.

Gastil, John, E., Pierre Deess, Philip J. Weiser, and Cindy Simmons.
*The Jury and Democracy: How Jury Deliberation Promotes Civil
Engagement and Political Participation.* Oxford: Oxford
University Press, 2010.

Hale, Dennis. *The Jury in America: Triumph and Decline.* Lawrence:
University Press of Kansas, 2016.

Hamburger, Philip. *Is Administrative Law Unlawful?* Chicago:
University of Chicago Press, 2014.

Hamilton, Alexander, John Jay, and James Madison. *The Federalist.*
Edited by George W. Carey and James McClellan. Indianapolis:
Liberty Fund, 2001.

Hannaford-Agor, Paula, and Valerie P. Hans. "Nullification at Work?
A Glimpse from the National Center for State Courts Study of
Hung Juries." *Chicago-Kent Law Review* 78, no. 3 (2003): 1249–77.

Hans, Valerie P. *Business on Trial: The Civil Jury and Corporate
Responsibility.* New Haven: Yale University Press, 2000.

Hans, Valerie P., and Neil Vidmar. *Judging the Jury.* New York:
Plenum Press, 1986.

Hans, Valerie P., ed. *The Jury System: Contemporary Scholarship.*
Aldershot: Ashgate, 2006.

Jonakait, Randolph N. *The American Jury System.* New Haven: Yale
University Press, 2003.

Kalven, Harry, Jr., and Hans Zeisel. *The American Jury.* Boston:
Little, Brown, 1993.

Katz, Stanley N., ed. *The Case and Trial of John Peter Zenger.*
Cambridge, MA: Harvard University Press, 1989.

Kessler, Amalia D. *Inventing American Exceptionalism: The Origins of American Adversarial Legal Culture, 1800–1877*. New Haven: Yale University Press, 2017.

Langbein, John H. "The Disappearance of Civil Trial in the United States." *Yale Law Journal* 122 (2012): 522–72.

Langbein, John H. "On the Myth of Written Constitutions: The Disappearance of Criminal Jury Trial." *Harvard Journal of Law and Public Policy* 15.1 (1992): 119–27.

Langbein, John H., Renée Lettow Lerner, and Bruce P. Smith. *History of the Common Law: The Development of Anglo-American Legal Institutions*. New York: Aspen, 2009.

Larson, Carlton F. W. *The Trials of Allegiance: Treason, Juries, and the American Revolution*. New York: Oxford University Press, 2019.

Lerner, Renée Lettow. "The Surprising Views of Montesquieu and Tocqueville about Juries: Juries Empower Judges." *Louisiana Law Review* 81.1 (2020): 1–54.

Lerner, Renée Lettow. "The Troublesome Inheritance of Americans in Magna Carta and Trial by Jury." In Robert Hazell and James Melton, eds, *Magna Carta and Its Modern Legacy*, 77–98. Cambridge: Cambridge University Press, 2015.

Marder, Nancy S. "Batson Revisited." *Iowa Law Review* 97 (2012) 1585–1612.

Maxeiner, James R. *Failures of American Civil Justice in International Perspective*. New York: Cambridge University Press, 2011.

Millar, Robert Wyness. *Civil Procedure of the Trial Court in Historical Perspective*. New York: Law Center of New York University for the National Conference of Judicial Councils, 1952.

Oldham, James. *Trial by Jury: The Seventh Amendment and Anglo-American Special Juries*. New York: New York University Press, 2006.

Pizzi, William T. *Trials Without Truth: Why Our System of Criminal Trials Has Become an Expensive Failure and What We Need to Do to Rebuild It*. New York: New York University Press, 1998.

Storing, Herbert J., ed. *The Anti-Federalist: Writings by the Opponents of the Constitution*. Chicago: University of Chicago Press, 1985.

Sunstein, Cass R., Reid Hastie, John W. Payne, David A. Schkade, and W. Kip Viscusi. *Punitive Damages: How Juries Decide*. Chicago: University of Chicago Press, 2002.

Thomas, Suja. *The Missing American Jury: Restoring the Fundamental Constitutional Role of the Criminal, Civil, and Grand Juries*. New York: Cambridge University Press, 2016.

Thompson, Norma. *Unreasonable Doubt: Circumstantial Evidence and the Art of Judgment*. Philadelphia: Paul Dry Books, 2011.

Tocqueville, Alexis de. *Democracy in America*. Edited by J. P. Mayer. Translated by George Lawrence. New York: Harper Perennial, 1988.

Tunno, David. *Fixing the Engine of Justice: Diagnosis and Repair of Our Jury System*. Bloomington, IN: iUniverse, 2013.

Twain, Mark [Samuel Clemens]. *Roughing It*. New York: Oxford University Press, 1996.

Vidmar, Neil, and Valerie P. Hans. *American Juries: The Verdict*. Amherst, NY: Prometheus Books, 2007.

Witt, John Fabian. *Patriots and Cosmopolitans: Hidden Histories of American Law*. Cambridge, MA: Harvard University Press, 2007.

Trial lawyers

Abrams, Dan, and David Fisher. *John Adams under Fire: The Founding Father's Fight for Justice in the Boston Massacre Murder Trial*. New York: Hanover Square Press, 2020.

Abrams, Dan, and David Fisher. *Lincoln's Last Trial: The Murder Case That Propelled Him to the Presidency*. New York: Hanover Square Press, 2018.

Belli, Melvin M. *Melvin Belli: My Life on Trial*. New York: William Morrow, 1973.

Dekle, George R. Sr. *Prairie Defender: The Murder Trials of Abraham Lincoln*. Carbondale: Southern Illinois University Press, 2017.

Dirck, Brian R. *Lincoln the Lawyer*. Urbana: University of Illinois Press, 2008.

Farrell, John A. *Clarence Darrow: Attorney for the Damned*. New York: Vintage Books, 2012.

Hostettler, John. *Sir William Garrow: His Life, Times and Fight for Justice*. Sherfield on Loddon, U.K.: Waterside Press, 2011.

Steiner, Mark E. *An Honest Calling: The Law Practice of Abraham Lincoln*. DeKalb: Northern Illinois University Press, 2006.

Wilkie, Curtis. *The Fall of the House of Zeus: The Rise and Ruin of America's Most Powerful Trial Lawyer*. New York: Crown, 2010.

Jurors around the world

Almeida, Vanina G., Denise C. Bakrokar, Mariana Bilinski, Natali D. Chizik, Andrés Harfuch, Lilián Andrea Ortiz, Maria Sidonie Porterie, Aldana Romano, and Shari Seidman Diamond.

"The Rise of the Jury in Argentina: Evolution in Real Time."
In Sanja Kutnjak Ivković, Shari Seidman Diamond,
Valerie P. Hans, and Nancy S. Marder, eds, *Juries, Lay Judges,
and Mixed Courts: A Global Perspective*. Cambridge: Cambridge
University Press, 2021, 25–46.

Bedford, Sybille. *The Faces of Justice: A Traveller's Report*. New York:
Simon & Schuster, 1961.

Casper, Gerhard, and Hans Zeisel. "Lay Judges in the German
Criminal Courts." *The Journal of Legal Studies* 1 (1972): 135–91.

Daumier, Honoré. *Lawyers and Justice*. Boston: Boston Book and Art
Shop, 1971.

Donovan, James M. *Juries and the Transformation of Criminal
Justice in France in the Nineteenth and Twentieth Centuries*.
Chapel Hill: University of North Carolina Press, 2010.

Esmein, Adhémar. *A History of Continental Criminal Procedure*.
Translated by John Simpson. London: John Murray, 1914.
Gleadow, Carmen. *History of Trial by Jury in the Spanish Legal
System*. Lewiston, NY: Edwin Mellen Press, 2000.

Ivković, Sanja Kutnjak, Shari Seidman Diamond, Valerie P. Hans, and
Nancy S. Marder, eds. *Juries, Lay Judges, and Mixed Courts:
A Global Perspective*. Cambridge: Cambridge University Press, 2021.

Johnson, David T., and Dimitry Vanoverbeke. "The Limits of Lay
Participation Reform in Japanese Criminal Justice." *Hastings
Journal of Crime and Punishment* 1, no. 3 (2020): 439–85.

Langbein, John H. "Mixed Court and Jury Court: Could the
Continental Alternative Fill the American Need?" *American Bar
Foundation Research Journal* 1981, no. 1 (1981): 195–219.

Lerner, Renée Lettow. "The Intersection of Two Systems: An
American on Trial for an American Murder in the French *Cour
d'assises*." *University of Illinois Law Review* 2001, no. 3 (2001):
791–856.

Montesquieu, Charles de Secondat, baron de. *The Spirit of the Laws*.
Translated and edited by Anne M. Cohler, Basia Carolyn Miller,
and Harold Samuel Stone. Cambridge: Cambridge University
Press, 1989.

Offit, Anna. "Dismissing the Jury: Mixed Courts and Lay Participation
in Norway." In Sanja Kutnjak Ivković, Shari Seidman Diamond,
Valerie P. Hans, and Nancy S. Marder, eds, *Juries, Lay Judges,
and Mixed Courts: A Global Perspective*. Cambridge: Cambridge
University Press, 2021, 197–217.

Park, Jaihyun. "The Korean Jury System: The First Decade." In Sanja Kutnjak Ivković, Shari Seidman Diamond, Valerie P. Hans, and Nancy S. Marder, eds, *Juries, Lay Judges, and Mixed Courts: A Global Perspective*. Cambridge: Cambridge University Press, 2021, 88–106.

Sharafi, Mitra. *Law and Identity in Colonial South Asia*. Cambridge: Cambridge University Press, 2014.

Thaman, Stephen C. "Europe's New Jury Systems: The Cases of Spain and Russia." *Law and Contemporary Problems* 62, no. 2 (1999): 233–59.

Thaman, Stephen C., ed. *World Plea Bargaining: Consensual Procedures and the Avoidance of the Full Criminal Trial*. Durham, NC: Carolina Academic Press, 2010.

Turner, Jenia I. *Plea Bargaining Across Borders*. New York: Aspen, 2009.

Vanoverbeke, Dimitri. *Juries in the Japanese Legal System: The Continuing Struggle for Citizen Participation and Democracy*. Abingdon, U.K.: Routledge, 2015.

Vidmar, Neil, ed. *World Jury Systems*. Oxford: Oxford University Press, 2000.

Fiction

Grisham, John. *The Runaway Jury*. New York: Doubleday, 1996.
Lee, Harper. *To Kill a Mockingbird*. Philadelphia: J. B. Lippincott, 1960.
Sayers, Dorothy L. *Strong Poison*. London: Gollancz, 1930.

Films

Desai, Dharmendra Suresh, director. *Rustom*. Zee Studios, 2016. 2 hr, 28 min.
Fleder, Gary, director. *The Runaway Jury*. 20th Century Fox, 2003. 2 hr, 7 min.
Lumet, Sidney, director. *12 Angry Men*. United Artists, 1957. 1 hr, 36 min.
Lumet, Sidney, director. *The Verdict*. 20th Century Fox, 1982. 2 hr, 9 min.
Lynn, Jonathan, director. *My Cousin Vinny*. 20th Century Fox, 1992. 1 hr, 59 min.

Mulligan, Robert, director. *To Kill a Mockingbird*. Universal Pictures, 1962. 2 hr, 9 min.

Preminger, Otto, director. *Anatomy of a Murder*. Columbia Pictures, 1959. 2 hr, 40 min.

Schepisi, Frederic, director. *A Cry in the Dark* (released as *Evil Angels* in Australia). Warner Bros., 1988. 2 hr, 1 min.

Wilder, Billy, director. *Witness for the Prosecution*. United Artists, 1957. 1 hr, 56 min.

Zaillian, Steven, director. *A Civil Action*. Buena Vista Pictures, 1998. 1 hr, 55 min.

Index

Index

PHILOSOPHY OF LAW
A Very Short Introduction
SECOND EDITION
Raymond Wacks

The concept of law lies at the heart of our social and political life. Legal philosophy, or jurisprudence, explores the notion of law and its role in society, illuminating its meaning and its relation to the universal questions of justice, rights, and morality.

In this *Very Short Introduction* Raymond Wacks analyses the nature and purpose of the legal system, and the practice by courts, lawyers, and judges. Wacks reveals the intriguing and challenging nature of legal philosophy with clarity and enthusiasm, providing an enlightening guide to the central questions of legal theory.

In this revised edition Wacks makes a number of updates including new material on legal realism, changes to the approach to the analysis of law and legal theory, and updates to historical and anthropological jurisprudence.

www.oup.com/vsi